Truth, Lies and Trust on the Internet

The Internet is often presented as an unsafe or untrustworthy space: where children are preyed upon by paedophiles, cannibals seek out victims, offline relationships are torn apart by online affairs and where individuals are addicted to gambling, love, and cybersex.

While many of these stories are grounded in truth, they do paint a rather sensationalised view of the Internet, the types of people who use it, and the interactions that take place online. Simultaneously, researchers claim that the Internet allows individuals to express their true selves, to develop 'hyperpersonal' relationships characterised by high levels of intimacy and closeness. At the heart of these competing visions of the Internet as a social space are the issues of truth, lies and trust.

This book offers a balanced view of the Internet by presenting empirical data conducted by social scientists, with a concentrated focus on psychological studies. It argues that the Internet's anonymity, which can enable, for instance, high levels of self-disclosure in a relationship, is also responsible for many of its more negative outcomes such as deception and flaming. This is the first book to develop a coherent model of the truth–lies paradox, with specific reference to the critical role of trust.

Truth, Lies and Trust on the Internet is a useful text for psychology students and academics interested in Internet behaviour, technology and online deviant behaviour, and related courses in sociology, media studies and information studies.

Monica Whitty is senior lecturer in the Division of Psychology at Nottingham Trent University. She lectures on cyberpsychology, social psychology, and qualitative methods. In recent years her work has focused on online dating, cyber-relationships, Internet infidelity, misrepresentation of self online, cyber-stalking, cyber-ethics, and Internet and e-mail surveillance in the workplace.

Adam Joinson is senior lecturer in Information Systems at the School of Management, University of Bath. His research interests include computer mediated communication, e-social science, privacy and disinhibition online.

Truth, Lies and Trust on the Internet

Monica Whitty and Adam Joinson

Routledge
Taylor & Francis Group

LONDON AND NEW YORK

First published 2009 by Routledge
27 Church Road, Hove, East Sussex BN3 2FA

Simultaneously published in the USA and Canada
by Routledge
270 Madison Avenue, New York NY 10016

*Routledge is an imprint of the Taylor & Francis Group, an Informa
business*

Copyright © 2009 Psychology Press

Typeset in Times by Garfield Morgan, Swansea, West Glamorgan
Printed and bound in Great Britain by TJ International Ltd, Padstow,
Cornwall
Cover design by Hybert Design

This publication has been produced with paper manufactured to strict
environmental standards and with pulp derived from sustainable
forests.

Please note: websites referenced in this book may
contain sexually explicit imagery that some may find
offensive or disturbing.

British Library Cataloguing in Publication Data
A catalogue record for this book is available from the British Library

Library of Congress Cataloging-in-Publication Data
Whitty, Monica T., 1969-
   Truth, lies and trust on the Internet / Monica Whitty and Adam
Joinson.
      p. cm.
   Includes bibliographical references and index.
   ISBN 978-1-84169-584-6 (hardcover)
   1. Internet users–Psychology. 2. Internet–Psychological aspects. 3.
Internet–Social aspects. 4. Cyberspace–Psychological aspects. 5.
Social psychology. I. Joinson, Adam N., 1970- II. Title.
   HM1017.W45 2009
   303.48'33–dc22
                                                    2008004061

ISBN 978-1-84169-584-6

Contents

Tables

Figures

1 Introduction

The number of people who have access to the Internet and the number of hours people spend online are still increasing. Its form continues to change and develop. Fads come and go. New online communities emerge, some old ones remain. Relationships are initiated and developed and people break up on the Internet.

Scholars across a variety of disciplines have studied how people interact online, their expectations of how this space should work, how it sometimes disappoints, and how it sometimes pleasantly surprises. Some scholars have taken the position that people lie more online than any other medium, while others have argued that people are more honest in this space. So which is it? Are people more dishonest or honest on the Internet? In this book we take the position that it is both.

Our book presents what we believe to be the truth–lies paradox of the Internet. We do this via a psychological lens, while still drawing from a variety of disciplines. We argue that researchers need to acknowledge that both openness and deceit are encouraged online. At the heart of these competing visions of the Internet as a social space, we also argue that we need to consider how trust plays a role. Without trust the Internet would look very different to how it currently operates.

This book begins by considering truth. In the following chapter we do so by examining self-disclosures on the Internet. Chapter 2 highlights the literature which has demonstrated that people are more likely to disclose information about themselves on the Internet compared to equivalent face-to-face (FtF) encounters. Often these self-disclosures are very secret aspects of a person's life (e.g. their sexual preferences). Knowing that people self-disclose more online is not only important in helping researchers understand online interactions, but also useful for those wanting to conduct their research in this space. Doing so could possibly reveal a different truth than perhaps administering a survey FtF (a notion we take up further in Chapter 5).

In Chapter 2 we also claim that how much is self-disclosed on the Internet depends on where people are communicating and with whom they are sharing their intimate details. For instance, many studies have shown that people are more likely to self-disclose when they are anonymous and when they are talking to strangers on the Internet. In contrast, we would expect self-disclosure in social networking sites such as MySpace, Bebo and Facebook to be different, given that often the audience is typically known to the person self-disclosing. Weblogs (personal online diaries) again probably set a different scene for self-disclosures given their structure and purpose.

Self-disclosing more or being 'hyperhonest' can be beneficial in a number of ways. It can allow an individual to unburden themselves. It can be cathartic or therapeutic. Moreover, it can bring about stronger connections with others online which often leads to close friendships and romance. Being too honest though can have a price to pay as it can drive some people away (e.g. being too honest about one's negative aspects on an online dating profile).

In Chapter 3 we go into more detail as to how being hyperhonest about oneself can lead to budding relationships on the Internet. Here we point out that the initial limitations people believed would prevent close relationships developing online were quickly overcome. This is because individuals learnt alternative ways to express themselves and their true feelings for others without the use of non-verbal cues we so often rely upon (even if they do this often unconsciously).

The type of self we present to others can make a difference as to whether a relationship will progress in cyberspace. In Chapter 3 we demonstrate that this is also dependent on which online space individuals meet in. For instance, in newsgroups and chat rooms, presentations of a more 'inner truth' can lead to close relationships that have been known to move successfully offline. However, this is not the case for dating sites. Instead, online daters who present a more accurate presentation of their everyday selves are more likely to get beyond the first date.

Some people arguably benefit more from the unique space that is cyberspace. Shy and socially anxious individuals have been found to prefer many spaces online to get to know others. In particular, it has been found that shy people enjoy meeting potential romantic partners in newsgroups and on online dating sites.

Does telling greater truths online have any other benefits than simply developing close relationships? In Chapter 4 we make the claim that the Internet does provide new benefits for people and that psychologists should be especially interested in knowing more about these benefits. We begin the chapter by noting the early research which argued that the Internet caused people to become lonely and that weak ties were detrimental rather than helpful. We then proceed to consider the research which rebutted these initial claims and presented the alternative view that weak ties can be helpful and that people can feel genuinely supported by others on the Internet. In contrast to the view that the Internet makes people lonely is the view that lonely people benefit from their online social encounters. In order to benefit from the Internet, however, users need to know how to use it and feel confident in their ability; that is, they need to be high in Internet self-efficacy.

Chapter 4 also considers online social support groups. Some of these are set up by experts, while others are run by laypeople. Either way, the support available via these groups is typically both informational and empathetic. Support groups have been set up for a range of problems, from medical through to disabilities and psychological difficulties. It is no wonder that people are flocking to these sites. Despite the many benefits that these online social support groups offer, the negative consequence of signing up to them also needs to be considered. For example, some sites provide misinformation, sometimes there is conflict amongst group members and some people may become too reliant on this form of support. Given this, more research is clearly required to ensure people gain the most from online support groups.

In Chapter 5 we discuss how researchers might best use the Internet to recruit participants and examine psychological and social issues. In this chapter we point out research that has found that individuals often admit to socially undesirable behaviours online more than they would FtF. Moreover, they are more likely to disclose sensitive information about themselves on a computer compared to traditional pencil and paper surveys. Importantly, however, it is pointed out here that this heightened truthfulness in online research environments is not guaranteed and that there are certain techniques researchers need to be aware of if they are hoping to obtain greater self-disclosure via online research methodologies. For example, people have to believe they can trust the site where they are answering the survey and the researchers who are conducting the study.

In addition to knowing the optimal conditions for conducting research online, scholars need to be ensuring that they conduct their research in an ethical manner. Chapter 5 also considers ethical issues pertinent to online research. For example, how do we still ensure informed consent, ability to withdraw consent, confidentiality and debriefing? These questions need to be considered in light of the online space being researched. For example, we make the case that moderated sites ought to acquire the consent of both the participants and the moderators who run the site (as one would with any offline organisation). While organisations are rewriting their ethical guidelines (e.g. The British Psychological Society) there still is not total consensus. Future researchers of the Internet will obviously need to adhere to new guidelines as well as reflect on their practices to ensure they are conducting ethical research.

As we pointed out at the beginning of this chapter, this is not a book simply about truth on the Internet. The other side of the coin, deceit and dishonesty, is equally important for researchers to acknowledge and consider. Chapters 6 through to 8 consider the variety of ways in which individuals misrepresent themselves and blatantly lie on the Internet. Chapter 6 examines the numerous types of online deception and how this has impacted on individuals and online communities. We especially focus on two forms of deception – identity-based and message-based deception. Identity-based deception, for example, might involve pretending to be a legitimate member of a group or gender-switching. Message-based deception, in contrast, involves the content of the communication (e.g. lying to one's spouse about being at work when one is really in the pub having a couple of pints).

As we illustrate in Chapter 6 some lies told online can have costly consequences for those who are taken in by the lie. Phishing, for instance, tricks people into handing over information which allows scammers to break into their bank accounts. Another more fairly well known scam, named the Nigerian e-mail scam, has not only cost people money but sometimes their lives. Readers will be pleased to know, however, that there are strategies they can employ in an attempt to work out whether they are being lied to.

Are people more likely to lie on the telephone, FtF or on the Internet? In Chapter 6 we consider this question. We examine a number of theories that have been devised to explain lying behaviour, including social distance theory, media richness theory and features-based theory. We also look at empirical studies that have been conducted to test out these theories. While the research is still fairly scant, it seems that not only do we need to consider the communication medium, but also the type of lie and the target of the lie.

Chapter 7 considers lying on online dating sites. We examine here the more common types of misrepresentation evident on such sites. For example, on the profiles people construct for these sites individuals often lie or exaggerate about their looks, personality, age, intentions, socio-economic status and relationship status. Given that online daters are aware that others misrepresent themselves on these sites, as discussed in this chapter, individuals look for 'indicators of trust' to help decide whether the potential date is worthwhile getting to know further offline. For example, cliché-type profiles were often overlooked by online daters. The screening out process for online daters, however, continues offline. As this chapter illustrates, the first FtF meeting is more a checking exercise than a traditional first date. If the online dater matches up to their profile, the relationship then progresses after this date in a more traditional sense.

Do people intentionally lie on online dating sites? In Chapter 7 we consider whether people are telling out-and-out lies or instead presenting a different self online. This chapter also examines which version of the truth is more likely to lead to budding romantic relationships. However, we also highlight here a much more malicious type of lie told by some on these sites. This is known as the 'romance scam', which is another version of the Nigerian e-mail scam. Given that it is a fairly new scam, it has been known to catch out quite a number of unsuspecting online daters.

In Chapter 8 we look at how people have lied online about their status or kept their online interactions a secret from their offline partner. This is what psychologists refer to as Internet infidelity, which is widely agreed to be a real form of betrayal. As we demonstrate in this chapter, online relationship transgressions can be both sexual and emotional. For example, sexual acts can include cybersex, hot chatting and flirtation. Emotional betrayal might include falling in love with someone online or sharing intimate details about oneself. In this chapter we also consider why these behaviours might be considered as real forms of cheating. Individuals have also been known to seek out others online in order to engage in offline affairs. In Chapter 8 we also look at online sites which have been set up to assist individuals looking for an offline affair.

When it comes to offline betrayal, research often finds that men are more upset by sexual transgressions, while women are more upset by emotional transgressions. In Chapter 8 we examine whether research to date has found similar gender differences with Internet infidelity. This chapter considers theories, such as the evolutionary theory and double-shot hypotheses, which attempt to account for these gender differences.

Issues of trust are considered throughout the book. Nonetheless, we felt it important to consider trust in more detail, given that trust is of the utmost importance if relationships and communities are to exist online. The research on trust online makes a distinction between trusting people and trusting online features (e.g. trusting a website, an online questionnaire or online casino). In addition, as highlighted in this book, people use the Internet for a range of activities that require trust, such as banking, shopping, running businesses and engaging in work activities.

In Chapter 9 we argue that trust is multidimensional. In this chapter we discuss how individuals build trust in interpersonal computer mediated communication. For example, people go about reducing uncertainty about others online by asking direct probing questions. In turn, to instil trust in others people self-disclose in more detail than they would normally FtF and provide photographs about themselves to establish credibility. We also look at how people trust online places which on the surface would appear highly risky to trust. For example, eBay is risky for both sellers and buyers to trust and yet it is a highly successful place for individuals to trade and buy goods. We look at how this site has managed to earn such a good reputation. The types of online websites that are more trustworthy are also considered in this chapter. Moreover, it might surprise some to know that people often make up their minds about the trustworthiness of a site within milliseconds.

Chapter 10 highlights another dark side of online interactions – that of cyber-harassment and cyberstalking. In this chapter we show the difficulties in trusting that others will not harass us online or use the Internet to locate us in order to harass us offline. This chapter presents a number of case studies to illustrate the different ways that individuals have been known to be stalked or harassed online. For example, some individuals who have experienced unrequited love have been known to spread vicious and untrue rumours on the Internet as revenge. Organisations have also suffered as a consequence of untruths told about them online. These lies can be spread very quickly in cyberspace. Fortunately, many countries are formally recognising cyber-harassment and cyberstalking as 'real' crimes and legislation has been written to deal with this criminal activity. Moreover, given that cyber-harassment can occur within work organisations, workplaces are starting to develop cogent policies in an attempt to obviate this problem. The problem for organisations, however, is that their employees can be cyber-harassed by people from outside the organisation.

In Chapter 11 we argue that some people trust others a little too readily on the Internet. This chapter warns people about how online privacy can be quickly eroded. This relates to a number of different types of privacy: for example, informational privacy, accessibility privacy and expressive privacy. Our privacy online can potentially be invaded not only by strangers but also by family and friends. Moreover, software has been specifically designed to make it easy to do so. For example, online monitoring software is being marketed for those who do not trust their spouses. One can monitor not only which sites their spouses visit but every word their spouses write in cyberspace, be that in e-mail, newsgroups, Instant Messenger, and so forth.

In Chapter 11 we make the argument that because of changes in society and technology, what would be considered acceptable surveillance has altered in recent times. For example, it is fairly common for individuals to run a Google search on someone they have just met. Moreover, workplaces these days are more likely to believe that it is acceptable to monitor their workers – even without their knowledge. This attitude obviously affects employees, many of whom are unhappy with having their employers spying on their Internet activities.

The link between privacy and trust is considered in more detail in Chapter 12. This chapter considers online counselling and the need for both clients and therapists to trust one another in cyberspace. Without this trust, online therapy would obviously be impossible. Online counselling comes in many forms. There have even been computer programs developed to conduct counselling. These programs are still quite crude, but there is the possibility that more sophisticated systems could replace human counsellors in the future. Perhaps more important, however, is the fact that online counselling is reaching a wider range of people in need – those who perhaps could not afford offline counselling and those who would not have sought out counselling had it not been for the Internet. Nonetheless, therapists need to take into account that online counselling is not for everyone. Finally, this chapter considers key aspects of online counselling that therapists need to consider in more depth – from practicalities such as legal implications to options such as avatar therapy.

In many ways the Internet is a very different medium from, for example, the telephone and FtF. What makes this space unique is how we communicate within it. As we illustrate in this book, often our communication is 'hyperhonest' and paradoxically it is often 'hyperdishonest'. These two contrasting features should be of concern for scholars, web designers and of course the users of the Internet. Moreover, how people manage to trust this space and how much their trust is justified cannot be ignored. We hope that by the time you, the reader, get to the end of this book you too will have a better understanding of the importance of understanding truth, lies and trust on the Internet.

2 Let's talk about me, me, me

Self-disclosure on the internet

> There are only two ways of telling the complete truth – anonymously and posthumously.
>
> (Thomas Sowell 1930)

Sometimes it is easier to tell the truth to strangers than to close friends or family. In fact, quite often people go to extreme lengths to hide information from those close to them, while simultaneously confiding in strangers. This is what psychologists refer to as the 'stranger-on-the-train phenomenon' (discussed in more detail in Chapter 3). In this chapter, we look at self-disclosure on the Internet – what it is and how it is measured, how being online influences it and the possible implications for people's well-being.

Self-disclosure is the telling of the previously unknown so that it becomes shared knowledge, the 'process of making the self known to others' (Jourard and Lasakow 1958: 91). The converse of self-disclosure is secrecy, keeping personal information to ourselves. However, not all self-disclosure is equal – especially when online. Disclosing one's age, sex and location in response to the query ('a/s/l?') is not equivalent to disclosing a deeply held fear or vulnerability. Self-disclosure is also best understood within the context of a specific interaction; that is, when thinking about disclosure, it is important to recognise the recipient as well as the protagonist. Often, disclosure needs to be 'brought off' (Antaki *et al.* 2005). For instance, let's imagine that the disclosure we are thinking about making requires declaring our feelings to a person we find attractive. This kind of disclosure has all sorts of attendant risks: we could be humiliated; the person we are disclosing to could then tell other people; we could even be overheard making the disclosure. So, when thinking about making a disclosure of this kind, we need to be acutely aware of the environment, the recipient's likely response and the possible longer term consequences. It is hardly surprising then that the person doing the disclosing will attempt to control the encounter in as many ways as possible. One solution could be to move the interaction to a 'leaner' medium – that is, one with fewer cues, less opportunity to be overheard and a reduction in the impact of rejection. The telephone is an obvious example of a lean medium well suited to this kind of disclosure encounter. Fischer (1992) reports that in the early days of the telephone usage peaked when there was a young person in the house engaged in courtship. An alternative is to use a text-based communication medium, for instance SMS or e-mail. In a study of media choice in these kinds of situations, Joinson (2004) found that as the risk of rejection increased people were more likely to use e-mail over FtF modalities. But of course the choice of media by which to disclose is not so straightforward – e-mail and SMS introduce permanence, a record of the disclosure. For this reason, a non-permanent, text-based alternative (e.g. instant messaging or IM) would combine the benefits of both telephone and text-based interaction.

Self-disclosure has a number of other purposes. For instance, within dyads, particularly romantic relationships, it serves to increase mutual understanding (Laurenceau *et al.* 1998), and builds trust by making the discloser increasingly vulnerable (emotionally or otherwise) to the other person (Rubin 1975). Since self-disclosure is often reciprocated, it serves to strengthen the ties that bind people in romantic or friendship-based relationships (Jourard 1971).

Disclosure within groups can serve to enhance the bonds of trust between group members, but it can also serve to legitimise group membership and strengthen group identity. For instance, the admission of a negative identity (e.g. 'I am an alcoholic') within a shared identity group serves both to increase trust by revealing a stigmatised identity, as well as acting as a membership card for a particular group (Galegher *et al.* 1998). Personal growth may be an outcome of honest self-disclosure (Jourard 1971). In a study reported by Pennebaker *et al.* (1988), participants assigned to a trauma-writing condition (where they wrote about a traumatic and upsetting experience for four days) showed immune system benefits, compared to a non-trauma writing group. Disclosure in this form has also been associated with reduced visits to medical centres and psychological benefits in the form of improved affective states (Smyth 1998). For people using the Internet to talk about their problems (or to publish weblogs), their activities may well have unforeseen, positive, health and psychological benefits. In fact, according to a recent survey (The Register 2006), almost half of Americans reported that using a blog acts as a form of therapy (it was the most popular reason cited for keeping a blog).

Finally, disclosure between an individual and an organisation can serve authentication purposes. This type of self-disclosure might establish identity, allow authentication of a claim to identity and enable an organisation to recognise you in the future in order to personalise its offerings to you. Organisations might also ask for personal information for marketing purposes; for instance, when registering to access a website or joining an online community. Of course, organisations in the form of researchers might also ask for personal information in the name of academic research.

New technology, and in particular the Internet, might well change the demands upon people to disclose personal information, as well as the possible implications of such disclosure. For example, disclosing personal information to another person online might not involve the increased vulnerability that usually follows self-disclosure of personal information offline (Ben-Ze'ev 2003). Organisations might also demand more information in the name of authentication (although this need not always be personal information). Furthermore, new technology changes the scope of personal information that can be disclosed or collected. The development of ambient and ubiquitous devices, such as smart mobile phones and RFID tags, makes it likely that information about location, movements and social interactions is likely to be collected in the future in some form. How we negotiate the disclosure of such information is a critical issue.

Self-disclosure and the Internet

Research over the last decade or so has established relatively clearly that people tend to disclose more information about themselves online compared to equivalent FtF encounters (Joinson and Paine 2007). Parks and Floyd (1996), for instance, studied the relationships formed by Internet users and found that people report disclosing significantly more in their Internet encounters compared to their real life relationships. Similarly, in a study of 'coming out on the Internet', McKenna and Bargh (1998) found that participation in online newsgroups gave people the benefit of 'disclosing a long secret part of one's self' (p. 682). Chesney (2005), in a small-scale study of online diaries, reported high levels of disclosure of sensitive information, with half of his participants claiming never to withhold information from their diaries.

There is also ample experimental evidence to support these claims. In the series of studies reported by Joinson (2001), the level of self-disclosure was measured using content analysis of transcripts of FtF and synchronous computer mediated communication (CMC) discussions (study one), and in conditions of visual anonymity and video links during CMC (study two). In keeping with the predicted effect, self-disclosure was significantly higher when participants discussed using a CMC system as opposed to FtF. In the second study, incorporating a video link while the participants discussed using the CMC program led to levels of self-disclosure similar to the FtF levels, while the comparison condition (no video link) led to significantly higher levels of self-disclosure.

Further empirical confirmation of increased self-disclosure during computer mediated communication (CMC) comes from the work of Tidwell and Walther (2002). They proposed that heightened self-disclosure during CMC may be due to people's motivation to reduce uncertainty. To test this, Tidwell and Walther recruited 158 students to discuss in opposite sex pairs with an unknown partner using a CMC system or FtF. The subsequent conversations were content analysed for disclosure using the breadth and depth indices developed by Altman and Taylor (1973). Tidwell and Walther found that those in the CMC condition displayed higher levels of both question asking and self-disclosure compared to the FtF condition. The questions asked by CMC discussants were also more probing and intimate than those asked by those talking FtF, while both the questions and disclosure by FtF interactants tended to be more peripheral than those in the CMC condition. Tidwell and Walther conclude that the limitations of CMC encourage people to adapt their uncertainty reducing behaviours – they skip the usual asking of peripheral questions and minor disclosure, and instead opt for more direct, intimate questioning and self-disclosure.

Surveys and research administered via the Internet, rather than using paper methodologies, have also been associated with reductions in socially desirable responding (Frick *et al.* 2001; Joinson 1999), higher levels of self-disclosure (Weisband and Kiesler 1996) and an increased willingness to answer sensitive questions (see Tourangeau 2004). In a similar vein, survey methodology techniques that tend to reduce human involvement in question administration also increase responses to sensitive personal questions. Compared to other research methods, when data collection is conducted via computer-aided self-interviews (where participants type their answers onto a laptop) people report more health-related problems (Epstein *et al.* 2001), more HIV risk behaviours (Des Jarlais *et al.* 1999), more drug use (Lessler *et al.* 2000), and men report less sexual partners and women more (Tourangeau and Smith 1996). Medical patients tend to report more symptoms and undesirable behaviours when interviewed by computer rather than FtF (Greist *et al.* 1973). Clients at a sexually transmitted disease (STD) clinic report more sexual partners, more previous visits and more symptoms to a computer than to a doctor (Robinson and West 1992). Ferriter (1993) found that pre-clinical psychiatric interviews conducted using CMC compared to FtF yielded more honest, candid answers. Similarly, automated or computerised telephone interviews, compared to other forms of telephone interviewing, led to higher levels of reporting of sensitive information (see Lau *et al.* 2003; Tourangeau 2004).

Conversely, methods that increase the social presence of the surveyor (e.g. by using photographs of the researcher) have been predicted to lead to a reduced willingness to answer sensitive questions (Tourangeau *et al.* 2003), although the findings of Tourangeau *et al.* were equivocal. However, Sproull *et al.* (1996) found that participants 'present themselves in a more positive light to the talking-face displays' (p. 116) than to text-only interfaces. Joinson *et al.* (2007) report that although personalising the research experience leads to higher response rates to a self-administered survey, it also reduces self-disclosure.

Different spaces, different audiences

The Internet is not a generic space and there is a multitude of audiences one might communicate with – some strangers, some known to us (Whitty

2007a, 2007b; Whitty and Carr 2006a). In light of the theories highlighted in this chapter, it would be fair to say that how much individuals self-disclose online and what they self-disclose will vary depending on the space and the audience.

Take, for example, social networking sites such as MySpace, Bebo and Facebook. These spaces are free services where anyone can set up a profile and communicate with people already known to an individual as well as find new people to communicate with. Individuals can post photographs, videos and audio files on their profile and provide details of their interests, hobbies and educational background. Users can even keep weblogs which detail what is going on in their daily lives. To communicate with others on these sites one can choose to e-mail others or communicate using Instant Messenger (IM) with one or more individuals. Individuals can invite others to be linked to their profile, making their network of friends public to others who come across their site. The people accepted into their network can leave messages on the site for others to see. Given that at least some of the people one would expect to visit and read one's profile on these sites are individuals known to the person offline, then one would expect fewer people to self-disclose intimate, private details. Moreover, one would expect that details about the individual would be far less exaggerated than, say for example, profiles on online dating sites (see Chapter 7). If one did, then one's friends could publicly challenge this information.

Weblogs are personal online journals or diaries that individuals update fairly regularly. These are kept for 'a number of reasons – sometimes to gain notoriety, sometimes for personal reasons (e.g., to keep friends up-to-date) and sometimes for professional reasons (e.g., journalistic purposes)' (Whitty and Carr 2006a: 4). Often the people who read a journal are again known to the person rather than strangers. Some researchers have considered self-disclosure and blogging. For example, Harper and Harper (2006) believe that blogging might encourage student self-disclosure. To investigate this they conducted a study where a small sample of 12 students was asked to participate in blogging in return for course credit. In focus groups where students were asked to debrief about their blogging experience, some of the participants felt that they disclosed more in their blog than they would have in the classroom. It is noteworthy, however, that most of this self-disclosure was descriptive (e.g. marital status and place of birth) – a type of disclosure that Harper and Harper acknowledge is the least risky form of self-disclosure. Perhaps this is because these individuals were writing for people who knew them well. There are a number of problems with Harper and Harper's study. They used a very small sample and students received credit for participating (and so might have felt coerced). However, the most important criticism that might be said about this study is that they compared blogging with a classroom, which is an environment where one would expect very little self-disclosure. It might have been more interesting, for example, to compare conversations which students had FtF in other situations.

Increased self-disclosure online is neither universal nor without its limits. Within the e-commerce sphere, many consumers have reported that being asked too much personal information has led to their withdrawal from a purchase (see Chapter 9). Paine *et al.* (2006) report that both people's general privacy concerns and their trust in the organisation collecting the information influence whether or not they provide sensitive personal information. Similarly, Andrade *et al.* (2001) report that although the reputation of a company and privacy policy can increase the likelihood of disclosure, the offer of financial reward decreases the likelihood that people will disclose.

For many online users, the self-presentation opportunities provided by the Internet mean that they are faced with a dilemma – visual anonymity may make candid self-disclosure easier, but it also enables people to put a 'gloss' on the information they provide. This is particularly acute in circumstances where both candid disclosure and positive self-presentation are of value, for instance in online dating. Whitty (in press a, 2007a) describes the tension between putting forward an attractive impression in online dating and the need to be honest about oneself, as well as the tensions between presenting an ideal versus an actual self. In a series of in-depth interviews, Whitty's participants described how they engage in strategic self-presentation when writing an online profile – often editing and changing their profile following time for reflection or considering the contacts made through their profile. This strategic self-presentation does, however, need to be grounded in reality, with clichéd or obviously exaggerated profiles filtered by users. Whitty (2007a) describes this as the 'BAR' approach – users need to achieve a balance between an 'attractive' and a 'real' self, such that their positive qualities are accentuated, but not falsified.

Models of self-disclosure on the Internet

Most models of self-disclosure online call upon anonymity in its various guises as the main explanation for the relatively high levels of self-disclosure seen on the Internet. 'This anonymity allows the persecuted, the controversial, and the simply embarrassed to seek information – and disseminate it – while maintaining their privacy and reputations in both cyberspace and the material world' (Sobel 2000: 1522). Anonymity online has a number of separate effects – it leads to a reduction in the number of cues available during interaction (sometimes called 'visual anonymity'), and it can also lead to a reduction in vulnerability due to lack of identifiability. These two different types of anonymity lead to quite different processes, although the outcome (increased self-disclosure) is the same.

Anonymity and self-disclosure

As noted earlier, visual anonymity gives people more control over their self-presentation online. While it may seem paradoxical that they should use this control to disclose information about themselves, there are a number of reasons why this might be the case. First, we are generally motivated to want people to have an accurate view of who we are. The early stages of a relationship might be characterised by a desire for the other person to see us in a positive light. As a relationship develops (whether friendship or romantic), this is replaced by a wish to be perceived accurately (Duck 1991).

Second, there might be an optimum level of intimacy during an interaction (Argle and Dean 1965). Because intimacy can be communicated in many different ways (e.g. eye contact, proximity and self-disclosure), an increase in one form of intimacy will lead to a reduction in another to redress the balance and restore the equilibrium. Thus, for instance, people reduce eye contact when they are about to discuss personal intimacies (Exline *et al.* 1965).

Third, people are also motivated to reduce uncertainty in an interaction. According to uncertainty reduction theory (URT, Berger and Calabrese 1975), people are motivated to reduce uncertainty in an interaction to increase predictability. In FtF interaction, uncertainty can be reduced through both verbal and non-verbal communication and cues. However, during CMC, uncertainty reducing behaviours are text based only, including increased levels of self-disclosure and question asking (Tidwell and Walther 2002).

Anonymity and self-awareness

Matheson and Zanna (1988) argue that evidence from CMC suggests that people may have increased private self-awareness and reduced public self-awareness during CMC. As greater self-disclosure is associated with heightened private self-consciousness (Franzoi and Davis 1985), this would suggest that computer users experience increased private self-awareness since we see increased self-disclosure online. Matheson and Zanna (1988) tested this notion in a study comparing the levels of self-awareness of 27 introductory psychology students discussing a topic using computers and 28 students discussing the same topic FtF. They found that 'users of computer-mediated communication reported greater private self-awareness and marginally lower public self-awareness than subjects communicating face-to-face' (p. 228). This would suggest that while self-presentation concerns are reduced (via lower public self-awareness), self-regulation and focus on internal states and standards may be enhanced (via higher private self-awareness). As noted earlier, Joinson (2001) has provided evidence that increased self-disclosure during CMC is due to increased private and reduced public self-awareness.

Changes in self-awareness online might also have other impacts. Sassenberg *et al.* (2005) examined the role of private self-awareness in attitude change during CMC. They found that the impact of media (CMC vs. FtF) on attitude change was mediated by private self-awareness; that is, reduced attitude change during CMC compared to FtF was dependent upon increases in private self-awareness during CMC. In a second study, they also found evidence that private self-awareness moderated the impact of medium on attitude change.

Vasalou *et al.* (2006) manipulated participants' private self-awareness while they played a trust game with what they thought was another person, but was actually a computer simulation. For those participants who betrayed the trust of the other remote participant, a high self-awareness trigger led to greater experience of shame and embarrassment, more likelihood that they would apologise and an increase in the amount of money they transferred in a subsequent round (a repair mechanism).

Hyperpersonal interaction and self-disclosure

According to Walther (1996), hyperpersonal interaction is created by four main factors. First, because many online communicants share a social categorisation they will also tend to perceive greater similarity between themselves and their conversational partner. As we tend to like those whom we see as similar, people communicating online will be predisposed toward liking their communication partners.

Second, the sender of a message can optimise their self-presentation; that is, they can present themselves in a more positive light than they might be able to FtF because they do not have to worry about their non-verbal behaviour. Walther recalls the phrase 'the waist is a terrible thing to mind' to argue that being freed from having to allocate scarce mental resources to controlling our visual cues and appearance means that we can allocate more to message construction – again leading to a more positive impression being conveyed to the receiver. Walther also suggests that being freed from concerns about our appearance might be linked to a heightening of focus on our own inner self. This would mean that messages sent during CMC would include more content on personal feelings and thoughts, and that the senders might be more in touch with their self-ideals (again helping with their self-presentation).

A third factor in hyperpersonal communication is the format of the CMC. Walther argues that asynchronous CMC (e.g. e-mail) is more likely to lead to hyperpersonal interaction because the communicants can: (a) devote a special time to CMC, rather than being distracted by other goings on; (b) spend more time composing/editing the message; (c) mix social and task messages; (d) avoid using up cognitive resources for answering immediately, thus paying more attention to the message.

The final factor Walther invokes is a feedback loop that causes these effects to be magnified through social interaction. In line with work on self-fulfilling prophecies and behavioural confirmation, as the interaction progresses so the inflated positive impressions will be magnified as the communicators seek to confirm their initial perceptions, and in turn respond to the positive impressions conveyed by their partners (Walther 1996).

Walther's theory of hyperpersonal communication relies on visual anonymity and asynchronous communication. Indeed, Walther (1999) warns against the trend to plug video cameras into PCs, arguing that visual cues detract from social impressions during CMC. For instance, Walther *et al.* (1999) report that long-term CMC groups show lower attraction and affinity if they have seen a still picture of their fellow participants.

Disinhibition and self-disclosure

Suler (2004a) has discussed in detail the 'disinhibition effect'. He has argued that sometimes people can reveal secret emotions, fears or wishes or they might be extremely kind online. This type of inhibition he refers to as 'benign disinhibition'. In contrast, he says that others might be extremely rude or very angry (e.g. flaming), or look at material which they might not look at otherwise, such as pornography. This he calls 'toxic disinhibition'.

Suler (2004a) identifies six main factors that lead to an 'online disinhibition effect', some previously well established, others based on psychoanalytic theory. These are: dissociative anonymity; invisibility; asynchronicity; solipsistic introjection; dissociative imagination; and minimisation of authority. Suler argues that anonymity online allows people to compartmentalise their online selves in the belief that their online behaviours 'aren't really me at all' (p. 322). Invisibility, according to Suler, is visual anonymity; that is, although many online interactants know each other, visual anonymity leads to a situation akin to the traditional psychotherapist sitting behind their client to encourage disclosure. Asynchronicity enables people to engage in 'emotional hit and run' – they do not need to face the immediate reaction to their behaviour. Meanwhile, solipsistic introjection is due to the lack of visual or verbal cues – Internet users read e-mail messages in their own voices in their heads, leading to processes of merging and possibly transference. When combined with dissociative imagination – that we can leave the imaginary world of the Internet behind when we switch off the computer – according to Suler we can also leave behind any responsibility for our behaviour in this different realm. Whitty and Carr (2005a) have argued that this is the case when it comes to Internet infidelity (see Chapter 8 for a more detailed discussion). Finally, Suler claims that the Internet causes the minimisation of authority, again encouraging disinhibited behaviour.

A privacy-based approach to understanding self-disclosure

Joinson and Paine (2007) have argued that the increased surveillance of Internet activities renders explanations based solely on anonymity unviable. Instead they have argued that we need to ask to whom is a user non-anonymous and in what form? For instance, the Internet and new media in general have tended to erode privacy through data mining, cookies, data footprints, and so on. Often the impression of privacy is a mirage. High levels of personal information are held by a number of gatekeepers – whether through the process of registration, caches and logs kept on various servers or even locally based records. It therefore becomes critical to be aware of the role of these gatekeepers in order to understand fully disinhibition online. Joinson and Paine (2007) propose that as well as looking at the micro-level impacts of the media environment on disclosure, one also needs to look at the macro-level – the wider context in which the micro-level behaviour is enacted. Specifically, Joinson and Paine identify trust, control and costs and benefits as critical to understanding any disinhibitory effect. Specifically, they point out that often we 'purchase' access to an environment in which we can act in a disinhibited manner by leaving our personal information with a trusted gatekeeper (e.g. a website owner via a registration form). Joinson and Paine argue that this enables users to purchase 'pseudonymity' – for instance, through the use of nicknames on a chat server.

A second process that Joinson and Paine identify relates to the costs and benefits of an activity. Many 'disinhibited' activities conducted online (e.g. cybersex, self-disclosure and accessing pornography) carry a cost in real life. Self-disclosure can make the discloser vulnerable to others, while accessing pornography can be a cause of embarrassment or shame. The Internet may well address this balance of costs and benefits by reducing the likely cost of a behaviour – disclosing secrets is easier if the recipient does not know who you are. Finally, Joinson and Paine consider that control is also a critical issue. Walther (1996) argues that hyperpersonal social interaction online occurs, at least in part, because of the increased control afforded by asynchronous, visually anonymous CMC. For instance, we can control what information we choose to disclose, in what manner and how we disclose it. By removing control from CMC (for instance, by introducing video or synchronicity), we also compromise privacy

Conclusions

As we will see throughout this book, truthful self-disclosure online is closely related not only to the attributes of the system (e.g. anonymity), but also to an individual's perception of the situation and their privacy concerns, the goal of the disclosure and factors related to the specific interactional dynamic (e.g. trust in the interaction partner or website). In the following chapter, we look more closely at one aspect of self-disclosure online, that of online dating, where the motivational goals of the users are potentially torn between being honest and being as desirable as possible.

3 The role of truth in relationship formation online

On 10 June 2006 *The Times* online ran a story with the title 'Romance with a Keyboard' (Stuttaford 2006). In this article the author recalls a story about a man whose wife left him without explanation. Rather than face up to his wife and ask her why she had left him, he instead decided to hack into her e-mail to discover that his wife had been using chat rooms and had left him to explore her lesbian tendencies. The abandoned husband decided to log on to the chat room and pretended to be a female professor of literature, seduced his wife, and finally took his vengeance by breaking up with her online. Stuttaford (2006) uses this story to warn us that 'you can never know who you are dealing with on the internet'.

On 8 June 2006 *The NewYorkBlade* ran a story with the title 'Online Hookup Sites See Thefts, Assaults' (LaPadula 2006). LaPadula (2006) reports the arrest of Wenzel, a 35-year-old man residing in the United States, who allegedly sought out dates or sexual encounters with gay men via the Internet. Wenzel allegedly set up these encounters so that he could steal from his Internet dates. At the time of his arrest he was also apparently wanted for several other crimes, including identity theft and credit card fraud. The warning reported in this article is that 'the anonymity of the internet is attractive to both customers and criminals . . . many of those who use online dating and hookup sites may be closeted gay men and may be reluctant to contact police when they fall victim to crime'.

As we illustrate in this book, stories about untruths told on the Internet are not uncommon. Moreover, there is a plethora of stories reported in the media, like those mentioned above, which caution users to beware of initiating relationships online and progressing them offline. These stories warn us of the predators and those that play with identities who inhabit this space. The questions we ask here are:

- Do these stories represent typical experiences of those going online to form relationships?
- Are people more dishonest to potential partners when romancing in cyberspace?
- Can real relationships initiate and develop in this space?

This chapter addresses these questions and makes the claim that real relationships do exist online and some successfully progress offline. Moreover, we suggest here that in many ways people can be more honest and open to their online friends and lovers.

Comparing online and offline communication

So how might communicating in cyberspace be different to other modes of communication such as telephone and FtF? In answering this question it is important to note that in the early days the Internet and the World Wide Web (WWW) were mostly spaces where individuals communicated to others via text. Pictures took a long time to download, and video, live streaming and audio files were rarely used. Unlike many of our other types of interactions, an important aspect of communication was missing – that of non-verbal cues and paralinguistic cues. Non-verbal cues include facial expressions and body language (e.g. smiles, grimaces, tiling the head and pointing), while paralinguistic cues are those that accompany speech, such as tempo, vocal pitch and intonation.

It has been argued that non-verbal cues play a critical role in our communication. Mehrabian and Ferris (1967) went so far as to propose that 'the combined effect of simultaneous verbal, vocal and facial attitude communications is a weighted sum of their independent effects – with the coefficients of .07, .38, and .55, respectively' (p. 252). Their rather conversational paper suggested that in FtF conversation 38 per cent of communication is inflection and tone of voice, 55 per cent is facial expression and only 7 per cent is based on the words that people say. Unfortunately, this statistic has grown into a widely spread urban myth. The formula was devised to explain a very narrow situation in which a listener analyses a speaker's general attitude towards that listener. Moreover, the experiments conducted consisted of individuals who had no prior acquaintance. Nonetheless, researchers since Mehrabian and Ferris's well-known work have demonstrated the importance of non-verbal cues in everyday communication. Given this, it is not surprising that Internet researchers have been very interested in what the effect of the absence of non-verbal cues has on our online communication and relating.

Although it might not seem immediately obvious, we also use non-verbal cues when chatting on the phone. We might display anger by raising our voice, sadness by lowering it or excitement by talking very quickly. Imagine the following statement said first in a sarcastic tone and second in a more excitable tone: 'I had a *really* good time at work today.' Depending on how we might put emphasis on the word 'really' can completely change the meaning of this statement. This is not so easy to do in text. Because of this, the early researchers into CMC did not hold out much hope for online relationships (e.g. Hiltz and Turoff 1978; Kiesler *et al.* 1984). Many early studies of mediated communication were grounded in theories which argued that a loss of visual cues led to a reduction in the socialness of an encounter. For instance, according to Sproull and Kiesler (1986):

> All communications media attenuate to at least some degree the social context cues available in face-to-face conversation. The telephone reduces dynamic and static cues by eliminating visual information about the communicators. Letters and memos reduce static cues by imposing standardized format conventions; they eliminate dynamic cues altogether.
>
> (pp. 1495–1496)

As such, one of the early predictions of work on CMC was that it would tend to be 'task-oriented', in that the medium is well suited to conveying plain information, but unsuitable for carrying socio-emotional information. For instance, Hiltz and Turoff (1978) reported that only 14 per cent of CMC groups' communication was socio-emotional in content, compared to 33 per cent in FtF groups. Rice and Love (1987) carried out an analysis on 2347 sentences exchanged between participants using CMC: 28 per cent were 'positive' socio-emotional messages, 4 per cent were negative socio-emotional messages and 71 per cent were task-oriented messages. This led to a widely accepted notion that CMC was suitable for task-oriented communication, but unsuitable for building socio-emotional ties (Rice and Love 1987). This assumption is still widely held (see, for instance, the work on trust in virtual teams discussed in Chapter 9 of this book).

Cyberspace is different in other ways too. Although many hundreds of people can inhabit this space simultaneously – playing online games, chatting in chat rooms or leaving messages on message boards – the physical presence of others is not immediately obvious. This again is especially the case when individuals are communicating via text. Moreover, many of the people we communicate with online are, at least initially, strangers. Often they are people we never intend to meet FtF. While this occurs offline too, for example when we encounter people on a plane or train, this meeting of strangers potentially occurs more frequently online.

Problems with online relating

Given the unique qualities of cyberspace, researchers have argued that it is difficult to initiate and develop 'real' relationships within this space. Theories such as social presence theory and social context cues theory, for instance, predict that online communication is less inhibited and that individuals are more likely to exhibit aggressive behaviours in cyberspace. Early CMC theorists enthusiastically adopted social presence theory, initially proposed by Short *et al.* (1976) to explain the 'most obvious defect of the simple telephone – the fact that one cannot see the other person or group' (p. 43). According to Short *et al.*, social presence is the 'salience of the other person in the interaction and the consequent salience of the interpersonal relationships' (p. 65). They argue that the 'capacity to transmit information about facial expression, direction of looking, posture, dress and non-verbal cues, all contribute to the social presence of a communications medium' (p. 65). So, for CMC, with not only the removal of visual cues but also vocal intonation, social presence is particularly low (almost akin to a business memo). In the case of the telephone, according to Short *et al.*, 'communication is intrinsically less sociable, more impersonal, and that, unless the task requires such psychological "distance", the mismatch is felt to be unpleasant' (p. 81).

The approach developed by Kiesler and her colleagues (e.g. Kiesler *et al.* 1984; Sproull and Kiesler 1986) is also based on the reduction in social cues when communicating by text. According to this model, social context cues are used to regulate social interaction, and in their absence people's behaviour will become uninhibited, anti-normative and focused on the self rather than the other person. Sproull and Kiesler (1986) note:

> Typically, when social context cues are strong, behaviour tends to be relatively other-focused, differentiated and controlled. When social context cues are weak, people's feelings of anonymity tend to produce relatively self-centred and unregulated behavior.
>
> (p. 1495)

Of course, anonymity also gives individuals more opportunities to misrepresent themselves in this environment and research finds that many people do misrepresent themselves online (e.g. Whitty 2002a; Whitty and Carville 2008). Given all of this, it is not uncommon for people to argue that intimacy is the last thing that CMC is suitable for.

Aggressive communication

A number of studies have demonstrated that aggressive communication occurs in online environments (e.g. Aiken and Waller 2000; Thompsen and Foulger 1996). This form of communication is often referred to as 'flaming'. More specifically, flaming has been defined as emotionally charged, hostile or insulting posts in CMC environments (Thompsen 1994). A flame is usually not intended to be constructive. Some researchers have attempted to categorise online insulting posts. For example, McLaughlin *et al.* (1995) have categorised offending posts into seven groups: (1) incorrect or novice use of technology; (2) bandwidth piggery; (3) violation of Usenet conventions; (4) violation of newsgroup conventions; (5) ethical violations; (6) inappropriate language; (7) factual errors. When flamers obviously set out to upset or offend other members of an online forum, or to begin irrelevant conversations, they are typically referred to as 'trolls'.

Researchers have found that under certain conditions flaming is more evident, or at least the text is perceived to be more aggressive. For example, in line with what social context cues theory would predict, Thompsen and Foulger (1996) found that e-mails with 'pictographs', or what are more commonly known as emoticons, reduced perceptions that communication involved flaming. However, this effect diminished in e-mails that were highly hostile. Importantly, other researchers have questioned the prevalence of 'flaming' (e.g. Lea *et al.* 1992).

Lost sense of community

In addition to pointing out the problems with the ways individuals communicate in cyberspace, some researchers have argued that the Internet is destroying offline community groups and voluntary associations (Putnam 1996, 2001). Putnam (2001) notes that Americans are far less active in their offline communities and posits that the surge in media consumption has contributed to this decline. He also suggests that the Internet is responsible for the falling social capital in the United States of America; that is, as Internet use increases, social trust and community participation decrease. Others have also expressed the concerns raised by Putnam. Some have contended that the Internet causes alienation and destroys community. As the Bad Subjects Production Team (1995) have expressed: 'like global capitalism, computer networks bring people together in alienation rather than solidarity'. The view is that the Internet is taking people away from 'good places' such as cafés, bars and local parks (see Hampton and Wellman 2003).

Real relationships on the Internet

Despite all the negative press that online relating has received, there is a plethora of academic papers which have shown that real friendships and real romantic relationships do initiate online and can move successfully offline. Others have contended that real communities can exist online (sometimes these are already established offline communities and sometimes new communities develop online). As we will discuss in more depth in Chapter 4, weak ties have their strengths.

Online relationships spark up in a number of different types of online spaces. Parks and Floyd (1996), for instance, found in their research on newsgroups that almost two-thirds of their sample (60.7 per cent) admitted to forming a personal relationship with someone they had met for the first time in a newsgroup. Of these, 7.9 per cent stated that this was a romantic relationship. In addition, they found that many of the relationships which began online also moved to interactions in other channels, including, for some, FtF. Parks and Roberts (1998) then attempted to replicate these results by examining relationships initiated and developed in MOOs (meaning multi-user dimension object oriented, which are spaces online where individuals connect to shared databases of rooms and other objects and typically interact in synchronous time). In their study they found that most of the participants they surveyed (93.6 per cent) reported forming at least one ongoing personal relationship during their time on MOOs. A variety of kinds of relationships were identified, including close friendships (40.6 per cent), friendships (26.3 per cent) or romantic relationships (26.3 per cent). Parks and Roberts (1998) remark that 'the formation of personal relationships on MOOs can be seen as the norm rather than the exception' (p. 529). Utz (2000) found in her study of multi-user dimension (MUD) users that 76.7 per cent of her respondents reported forming a relationship online that developed offline, of which 24.5 per cent stated this was a romantic relationship. In their examination of interactions in chat rooms, Whitty and Gavin (2001) found that many individuals form friendships and romantic relationships in this space.

How are real relationships formed online?

Early researchers were correct to note that CMC reduces the usual cues transferred in conversation, and that people can be anonymous in this space. So then, how is it that people manage to form real friendships and romantic relationships online? We believe that Joe Walther and his colleagues' research provides some clues as to why. Walther (1992) criticised early studies into CMC stating that these studies did not account for time. He found that if we observe how online groups communicate over time some important changes occur in the way individuals communicate and in the dynamics of the online group. Walther has suggested (1992, 1995) that the main difference between FtF communication and CMC is the pace at which relationships develop in each space rather than the capability to develop relationships. As Walther (1992) explains:

> Given sufficient time and message exchanges for interpersonal impression formation and relational development to accrue, and all other things being equal, relational (communication) in later periods of CMC and face-to-face communication will be the same.
>
> (p. 69)

Hence, the media might initially present hindrances because of the absence of certain cues traditionally expressed offline, but individuals are able to overcome these hurdles and adapt to their online environment. For example, individuals often employ emoticons, symbols to denote feelings or emotions, such as a smiley face ☺ or a wink ;-), or acronyms illustrating emotions (e.g. LOL which often represents 'laugh out loud') to display non-verbal cues that they would typically express in FtF settings. Other researchers have also found evidence for this. For example, Whitty (2004c) found that men and women were able to successfully translate the body using emoticons whilst flirting online.

Hyperpersonal communication

As Walther continued his work about online groups he discovered another interesting finding: not only do individuals overcome the initial hindrances they face in online communication, but also individuals sometimes experience intimacy and affection for their online partners that exceed those occurring in parallel FtF activities (Walther 1996). So much so, that some individuals tend to idealise their online partners. This, he argued, is because people can be quite strategic in the way they go about presenting themselves.

Walther *et al.* (2001) also believed that the types of strategies that individuals employ online and the expectations they may have play a pivotal role in the success or failure of online relating. For example, they found that displays of online affiliative behaviours depend on whether the individual anticipates a long-term or short-term commitment with their online partner. Moreover, the use of a visual medium also makes a difference. The presence of a photograph, for instance, prior to and during CMC had a positive effect on intimacy/affection and social attractiveness for short-term CMC partners. However, long-term CMC partners felt less intimacy/ affection and social attraction once a photograph was introduced, compared to CMC partners who communicated long term and had not seen a picture of each other. As we saw in the previous chapter, Internet communication has been associated with increased self-disclosure by a number of authors – perhaps in part due to the lack of visual cues.

Stranger-on-the-train phenomenon

It was mentioned earlier in this chapter that many of the people we meet online are strangers. Is this necessarily a bad thing? Obviously, it means that people might feel inclined to lie or exaggerate aspects about themselves, and perhaps even gender bend (see Whitty 2002a). However, looking at this in a more positive light, being anonymous allows individuals to explore their identity and potentially feel safer or less shy to flirt and develop relationships online (Whitty 2003a; Whitty and Carr 2006a).

Researchers have in fact found that there are certain advantages to communicating with strangers online. Parks and Roberts (1998), for example, have stated that individuals are more likely to self-disclose aspects about themselves to strangers online that one might not feel as comfortable doing FtF. They have compared this phenomenon to Thibaut and Kelley's (1959) 'stranger-on-the-train phenomenon'; that is, people feel more at ease revealing intimate aspects about themselves to someone they envisage they will never meet again. Hence, the Internet in some circumstances provides a space for individuals to be more emotionally open and honest (see Chapter 2). Being open and honest is of course important in relationship development. Paradoxically, as we argue in this book, it appears that the same aspects of the Internet that enable misrepresentation also encourage the development of relationships.

Presentation of possible selves on the Internet

The way individuals go about presenting themselves in cyberspace partly determines how successful their online relationships will be. This varies across different online spaces (Whitty 2007a; Whitty and Carr 2006a). In some places individuals reveal private aspects about themselves gradually (e.g. newsgroups) and in others they set out a detailed picture of themselves prior to any interaction (e.g. online dating sites).

Bargh *et al.* (2002) and McKenna *et al.* (2002) have been interested in which aspects of the self individuals are more likely to make known to others in non-visual anonymous environments such as newsgroups, as well as which presentations of self will lead strong Internet relationships. These authors have drawn from work on the 'true self' by Rogers (1951) and work on 'possible selves' by Higgins (1987) to consider which characteristics individuals typically present in newsgroups, and which presentation of self in newsgroups will more likely lead to long-term relationships that move successfully offline. They defined the true self (or what they also refer to as the 'Real Me') as traits or characteristics that individuals possess and would like to, but are not usually able to, express, and the actual self as traits or characteristics that individuals possess and express to others in social settings.

In considering these different presentations of self, McKenna *et al.* (2002) were interested in whether individuals who are better able to disclose their 'true' selves online than offline were more equipped to form close relationships online and then take these relationships offline successfully. To examine this, they randomly selected 20 Usenet newsgroups and asked the users to answer questions about their presentation of self and their online relationships. Their first study found that when people convey their 'true' self online they develop strong Internet relationships and bring these relationships into their 'real' lives. Two years after this initial study, 354 of the 568 participants were e-mailed a follow-up survey (the remainder of the sample had e-mail addresses that were no longer valid). In line with these researchers' prediction, these relationships remained relatively stable and durable over the two-year period.

Progression of online relationships

So how exactly do relationships initiate online and move to the offline world? The relationships that do progress offline typically do so in a series of steps. From chat rooms, newsgroups and discussion lists, individuals typically move to e-mail and spend some time getting to know one another via text, sometimes also using Instant Messenger, exchanging photos and using webcams. From there, if individuals feel they would like to know each other a little more, they might exchange phone numbers (usually mobile numbers) and then finally arrange to meet offline (McKenna *et al.* 2002; Whitty and Carr 2006a; Whitty and Gavin 2001). These steps represent increments of trust (Whitty and Gavin 2001).

Not all online relationships move offline, nor does everyone involved in an online relationship hope that their relationships will move to FtF encounters. Relationships that remain online or are trialled offline and then moved back to exclusively online are not necessarily less fulfilling than those relationships that naturally migrate to the offline world. For example, Whitty and Gavin (2001) found that quite a few of the chat room users they interviewed stated that some of the relationships they had decided to keep online were just as satisfying and 'real' as many of their offline relationships. For example, an 18-year-old they interviewed reported:

> It [the relationship] developed through an interesting chat on IRC and a series of about 500 e-mails. The attraction was merely someone who cared and listened. He was very sensitive and caring, and his picture was hot! [laughs] . . . we exchanged addresses and he sent me presents on Valentine's Day and Easter. We would write a two page e-mail every day, send sounds to each other, and eventually after six months we talked on the phone. Our phone conversation was very weak so we decided to stick to e-mail . . . We met after eight months of exchanging e-mails. He was a great guy, and it would have worked but he lived in e-mail. It was a good experience though and he was exactly like his photo.
>
> (Whitty and Gavin 2001: 628)

Types of online relationships

How a relationship progresses from the Internet is of course determined by what the individual is hoping to get from it. Progressing through increments of trust via various modes of communication might suit a couple who hope to move to a more long-term committed relationship. Griffiths (2001) has highlighted three types of online relationships. The first he describes as virtual ones. These couples develop a short-lived relationship and never meet FtF. Griffiths argued that such couples typically engage in sexually explicit text exchanges. The second type he suggests are those who intend to move from online to offline after becoming emotionally involved with each other. These relationships would progress gradually in the way that Whitty and Gavin (2001) describe. The third type of couple proposed by Griffiths meets offline but then due to geographical distance maintains the relationship online. A fourth type are those described in Whitty and Gavin's (2001) research – those who meet online and try to move the relationship offline only to find that the relationship works better online and so move it back to cyberspace.

Online dating

Another quite unique way of meeting online is via online dating sites. These sites offer yet another type of online progression. Online dating sites are similar to newspaper personals (but with much more information). On such sites an individual constructs a profile where they describe themselves and the type of partner they are looking for. They will also typically provide photographs of themselves and sometimes sound bytes and video. Users usually have to pay to use this service and once they identify a person whose profile they like, online contact is made through the system to gauge whether the other individual might also be interested. From there, individuals often organise to meet FtF.

We will be discussing online dating sites in more detail in Chapter 7. It is, however, noteworthy to mention briefly here that, as with other spaces online, researchers have been interested in how truthful individuals are to potential dates via online dating sites. They have also been interested in the types of presentation of self which are evident on these sites. The process of self-disclosure on online dating sites is very different to how potential couples open up about themselves when they meet in other online spaces or FtF (Whitty 2007a, 2007c, 2008). The 'social penetration theory', first proposed by Altman and Taylor (1973), suggests that relationships gradually move to greater levels of intimacy over time. Revealing too much about an aspect of the self that the other might disapprove of or not be interested in could bring the relationship to an abrupt end. Hence, the timing of how much one self-discloses is crucial to determining whether a relationship will continue to proceed. Rushing self-disclosure in the early stages of a relationship can seem unnatural and desperate (Lawson and Leck 2006). The self-disclosure evident on online dating sites is obviously quite different, given that individuals are expected to present both depth (e.g. stating one's political views) and breadth (e.g. what one does on the weekend) about themselves on their profiles (Whitty 2007a, 2008). Deciding what to present is therefore a tricky process. As you will see in Chapter 7, even though online dating sites are spaces where individuals are typically not visually anonymous (since they usually display a picture of themselves), some individuals have been known to misrepresent themselves on online dating sites – even about their physical appearance. It has therefore been argued that online daters who are more successful at progressing relationships beyond the site are those who create an attractive and interesting profile and one that is an accurate presentation of the self (Whitty 2007a, 2008).

The self that individuals choose to disclose on online dating sites needs to be an honest depiction of who they really are (as will be elaborated upon in Chapter 7). As some researchers have argued, this needs to be a self that can be objectively verified (Whitty 2007a; Yurchisin *et al.* 2005). Moreover, it needs to be a self that matches with their 'actual' personality – rather than the person one ideally sees themselves to be (Whitty 2007a, 2008). Not surprisingly then, online daters struggle with decisions about which strategies to employ when it comes to revealing aspects about themselves. While they understand they need to be honest, they are also savvy enough to know that they need to construct a profile which will stand out amongst the sea of other possibilities. In a way, online daters treat themselves and others as a commodity (Whitty 2007a; Whitty and Carr 2006a). Individuals need to think about what aspects of themselves will sell and what aspects in others they will buy into. Arvidsson (2006) has suggested that this process of 'branding' is akin to self-help ideology. The process of shopping on an online dating site has been nicely described by an online dater in previous work reported by Whitty and Carr (2006a: 131):

I   What are some of the differences and similarities you have found in meeting people through this online site and meeting people with other methods?

D   Really, I have found that, I suppose the RSVP women are really out there searching for, they are shopping. They have a person in mind and they are really looking to see what takes their eye or what stinks, but still looks ok. But they really are shopping. I use the VCR for example in this one in my own mind, while it has got a play and record, it's got to look good in the stereo cabinet.

(Danny)

What types of people are seeking out romance online?

Is everyone looking for love online or does a certain type of person prefer to seek out relationships in this space? Researchers have found that, in particular, the socially anxious and shy are often drawn to online spaces to initiate and develop relationships. It has been argued that this is because the Internet provides a safe, playful and less real space for individuals to try out relationships (Whitty 2007a; Whitty and Carr 2006a).

McKenna *et al.* (2002), mentioned early in this chapter, were interested in the types of people who were more likely to develop relationships via newsgroups. They especially focused their research on the more socially anxious and lonely individuals. Interestingly, they found that the more socially anxious and lonely were somewhat more likely to believe they could express their 'true' selves with others online than they could with people they knew offline. McKenna *et al.* (2002) conclude from this research:

Rather than turning to the Internet as a way of hiding from real life and from forming real relationships, individuals use it as a means not only of maintaining ties with existing family and friends but also of forming close and meaningful new relationships in a relatively nonthreatening environment. The Internet may also be helpful for those who have difficulty forging relationships in face-to-face situations because of shyness, social anxiety, or a lack of social skills.

(p. 30)

Other researchers have examined whether shy individuals are more drawn to online dating sites to seek out potential mates (e.g. Scharlott and Christ 1995; Whitty and Buchanan in press). Although dating sites have changed in structure over time and increased in popularity, shy people do seem to be attracted to this form of dating (Whitty and Buchanan in press).

Scharlott and Christ (1995) surveyed 102 registered subscribers to the online dating site Matchmaker in 1990. During the time they conducted their study individuals were visually anonymous on the site. The significant findings were that 'shyer users were more likely to agree that Matchmaker allows them to explore new aspects of their personality' and that 'seventy-four per cent of the high-shyness users indicated that their main purpose in using Matchmaker was to find a romantic or sexual relationship, while only 46 per cent of the low-shyness users answered that way' (Scharlott and Christ 1995: 199).

The structure of online dating sites has changed since Scharlott and Christ collected their data in 1990. An important difference is the use of photos and videos on these sites. Having a photo obviously makes one less anonymous and could potentially put off shy individuals. Given this difference, Whitty and Buchanan (in press) were curious to find out if this change, as well as the increased popularity of online dating, brought about a different population of online daters. They found that shy individuals were more likely to enjoy online dating as a method to seek out partners and more likely to use online dating sites compared to less shy individuals. Although they considered other characteristics, such as gender, sensation seeking, extraversion, and desire to initiate relationships, the only other significant findings were that older individuals prefer and use online dating sites more than younger individuals. The people who had already tried online dating were likely to continue with it, suggesting they still held out hope of finding a suitable partner via this method even if they had not yet had success.

The future of online romance

Individuals will no doubt continue to seek out and develop romantic relationships in cyberspace. However, in the future there will be new possibilities for how this will be achieved. While the background of literature on online partnering has to date mostly considered the meeting of strangers online, future research needs to consider how relationships initiate online between individuals already known to each other offline. For example, social networking sites (e.g. MySpace, Facebook and Bebo), and blogs where an individual places details about themselves and links themselves to people they know, have potential for romance to spark up. The types of information and presentation of self in these spaces are very different compared to other online spaces, especially when linked to others known to the person who can verify the information.

Cyberspace is arguably not restricted to just the Internet. As Whitty and Carr (2006a) report, Bluetooth technology is taking off as a new match-making tool. Some companies have even created matchmaking software for individuals' mobile phones. The software allows them to create a short profile and be alerted when a single person with the same software is in their proximity. In an interesting article reported on the BBC News site titled 'Phone Technology Aids UAE Dating', it was reported that all sorts of individuals are flirting and initiating romantic relationships via Blue-tooth technology (Sharp 2005). In this piece, Sharp reports that young men and women in conservative cultures such as the United Arab Emirates are setting up secret liaisons via their mobile phones. One young 20-year-old male she interviewed stated: 'In our country it's very rude to go up and talk to them [girls],' he says. 'I sent some notes, they liked them – they took my number and they called me. I say nice things – I'm into poems.'

Conclusions

To answer the questions first raised in this chapter, some people do lie to potential partners online – though we ought to recognise this also happens FtF. More importantly, real relationships do initiate in a variety of spaces online and many successfully move to offline spaces. How individuals present themselves on the Internet partly determines whether the relation-ship will endure. Furthermore, to date we find that the socially anxious and shy often prefer meeting others online. More and more people are using the Internet and the technology is developing so we can expect to find an increasing number of relationships budding and developing in cyberspace.

4 Misery loves company

Emotional and practical support online

The previous two chapters have established that people do open up more online. What psychologists have also questioned though is whether self-disclosing online is a healthy experience, especially for those who are not psychologically functioning optimally offline. In particular, psychologists have questioned whether the Internet is a therapeutic space for lonely individuals, or whether instead it makes people more lonely. Part of this debate has focused on the types of relationships or 'weak ties' that individuals form online, the suggestion being that 'strong ties' offline are of greater value. As we shall see in this chapter, some researchers have argued that when addressing these questions psychologists need to examine the full gamut of individuals' psychological make-up (e.g. personality traits), the types of places visited online and who individuals are communicating with. Given the growing number of online support groups, it is imperative that psychologists seriously question how helpful or unhelpful people's online ties really are. Moreover, as is demonstrated in this chapter, when considering online support groups, how the group is set up partly determines its success. This chapter will also examine a variety of types of online support groups and consider the strengths and weakness of these groups.

Does the Internet make people lonely?

In the early days of Internet psychology research, the general view was that too much use of the Internet led to negative outcomes. It was argued that the Internet could make people isolated, lonely and depressed. Early research supported this notion. For example, Kraut and his colleagues' (1998) well-known HomeNet study found that greater use of the Internet led to negative effects. These researchers conducted a longitudinal study in which they gave a computer, a free telephone line and free access to the Internet to 93 households (comprising a total of 169 individuals) who had never before accessed the Internet. During the course of the study, they tracked changes in psychological states over time. They found a significant relationship between heavy Internet usage and loneliness. Kraut *et al.* argued that since initial loneliness failed to predict subsequent loneliness, the most likely explanation was that increased use of the Internet was what caused the increase in loneliness. In other words, Internet usage was taking up time that could be better used for more psychologically beneficial interactions offline. Kraut *et al.* made the claim that online weak ties were being established which were of poorer quality compared to the types of relationships and strong ties already established offline.

It is noteworthy that Kraut *et al.*'s (1998) HomeNet study has been widely criticised. One of the major criticisms made is that they only used three items from the UCLA Loneliness Scale to measure loneliness and their Cronbach's alpha of .54 was clearly poor (Grohol 1998). Morahan-Martin (1999) also points out that the sample size was too small and not randomly selected. Perhaps a more important criticism, however, is that Kraut *et al.*'s findings might only explain novice Internet users (LaRose *et al.* 2001). The individuals who spent more time online in Kraut *et al.*'s study might have been simply ineffective users of the Internet and the stress of trying to work out how to use this new technology might have caused them to become more depressed (Whitty and McLaughlin 2007).

Interestingly, Kraut *et al.* (2002) found results contrary to their original study. In the three-year follow-up to the HomeNet study the same researchers found that almost all of the previously reported negative effects had dissipated. Instead, higher levels of Internet use were positively correlated with measures of social involvement and psychological well-being. Perhaps such results might be explained by LaRose *et al.*'s (2001) claim that it is also important to consider Internet self-efficacy (i.e. being confident and capable of using the Internet). Could it be that the participants in the HomeNet study became more Internet savvy over time, which in turn altered the way they used the Internet?

Others too, however, have noted that spending too much time online is associated with negative effects. Nie (2001) has found that Internet use can reduce interpersonal communication and lead to increased social isolation. He argues that part of the reason for this is because the Internet replaces other social activities, such as time spent with family and friends. Nie notes that other 'anti-social' activities, such as watching television, have not decreased for most people since they started using the Internet. Hence, people are not substituting one 'anti-social' activity for another, but are rather dedicating more hours in their everyday lives to engaging in socially isolated activities. Nie also believes that while watching television can be combined with other activities (e.g. just used as background noise), the Internet cannot and he also remarks:

> Many of us are familiar with that unique Internet characteristic of surfing that leads Internet junkies to sit down to do a single task and end up, hours later, with a loss of a sense of time, place, and original purpose.

> (Nie 2001: 431)

Sanders *et al.* (2000) surveyed 89 high school seniors about their levels of depression, Internet use and relationships with their mother, father and peers. They found that low Internet users (less than one hour per day), compared with high Internet users (more than two hours per day), reported better relationships with their mothers and friends. They did, however, find no significant differences between low and higher Internet users in respect to their relationship with their father or depression scores. Further research needs to look at what types of online encounters these high Internet users are engaging in.

Not all doom and gloom online

conflicting findings

Not all researchers agree with the above researchers' claims. Katz and Aspden (1997), for example, found from surveying 2500 individuals that Internet use had no apparent impact on offline social participation. Their research revealed that there were fewer socially isolated individuals among Internet users than non-users. Furthermore, Internet users were more likely to have recent social contacts and sources of information. Katz and Aspden argued that the Internet is a medium to cultivate friendships which often lead to meetings offline. They also claimed that 'Internet skills appear to be the most important determinant of friendship formation, eclipsing personality characteristics such as sociability, extroversion, and willingness to take risks' (Katz and Aspden 1997: 86). This would be in line with LaRose *et al.*'s (2001) theory on self-efficacy and Internet use (described above).

Others have also argued that individuals can benefit from weak ties. For example, Wellman (1997) argued that although strong ties provide more social support than weak ties, weak ties are not useless:

> Their very weakness means that they tend to connect people who are more socially dissimilar than those connected through strong ties. Consequently, weak ties tend to link people to other social worlds, providing new sources of information and other resources.
>
> (p. 196)

In research by Hampton and Wellman (2003: 304) it was found that Internet ties are '*not* a distinct social system'. Importantly, they found that online interactions can facilitate offline neighbourhood-based interactions. These results are in contrast to Putnam's views that the Internet would lead to a loss of community (as outlined in the previous chapter).

The contrasting view to the Internet causing loneliness is that lonely people have a greater desire to use the Internet and can even benefit from doing so. As Morahan-Martin and Schumacher (2003) have stated:

> The Internet provides an ideal social environment for lonely people to interact with others. Not only does it provide a vastly expanded social network, but also it provides altered social interaction patterns online that may be particularly attractive to those who are lonely.
>
> (p. 662)

To investigate this theory, Morahan-Martin and Schumacher surveyed 282 undergraduate students about their Internet use and behaviours and also obtained scores for loneliness. They found that, on average, lonely individuals used the Internet more on a weekly basis than did non-lonely individuals. The lonely also used e-mail significantly more hours per week than non-lonely individuals. The lonely were more likely than non-lonely to report that they used the Internet for the following reasons: to relax, for work, to meet people, for emotional support, talking to others who share the same interests and to waste time. Lonely individuals were more likely than non-lonely individuals to say that they preferred online communication to FtF communication. The lonely also found that cyberspace was liberating because they could be anonymous online. Furthermore, the lonely were more likely than the non-lonely to report that they liked the speed of communicating online and they have lurked online. Interestingly:

> Lonely users were more likely than non-lonely users to agree that when online: they were more themselves than in real life, they opened up more to people than in other forms of communication, they were friendlier, they had shared intimate secrets, and they had pretended to be someone else.
>
> (Morahan-Martin and Schumacher 2003: 665)

Overall, the lonelier individuals in Morahan-Martin and Schumacher's study reported feeling less inhibited, friendlier and more intimate online. Moreover, they claimed that their online friends were a source of emotional support and fun. What researchers have yet to determine, however, is whether the perceived benefits translate to real and long-term benefits.

It is also noteworthy that the link between online relating and loneliness is not restricted to western samples. More recent research examining a Japanese sample found support for the view that online friendships can be psychologically healthy (Ando and Sakamoto 2008). In their study, Ando and Sakamoto examined 187 undergraduate students based in Tokyo and Kyoto. They found that the participants who rated themselves low in physical attractiveness benefited from having a large number of cyber-friends. These individuals were more likely to feel less lonely and socially anxious as a consequence of gaining these online friendships. This would confirm the current more popular view that weak ties are psychologically beneficial.

Different personalities and online spaces

Hamburger and Ben-Artzi (2003) criticised Kraut *et al.*'s (1998) HomeNet study for not taking into account that the population of Internet users consists of a variety of personality types. They state:

> People use the Internet in a variety of ways in keeping with their own personal preference. Therefore, the results of this interaction between personality and Internet use are likely to vary among different individuals and similarly the impact on user well-being will not be uniform.
> (Hamburger and Ben-Artzi 2003: 71)

In their study, Hamburger and Ben-Artzi surveyed 85 Israelis about their Internet usage as well as obtaining scores for loneliness, extraversion and neuroticism. When it came to measuring Internet usage they considered three types of Internet services: social (chat, discussion groups and people–address seeking); information (work-related information and studies-related information); and leisure (sex websites and random surfing). Their results found that for men the use of Internet services was not related to loneliness, extraversion or neuroticism. In contrast, for women loneliness was significantly related both to neuroticism and the use of social Internet services. They argue that there are two possible explanations for this result. The first possible explanation is that Kraut *et al.* (1998) are correct in arguing that the Internet causes individuals (in this case women) to become more lonely. Their second explanation states:

> The use of the Internet social services is a result, and not a cause, of the increased loneliness of neurotic women, so that neuroticism increases, at least in the sense of negative affectivity, the feeling of loneliness, driving the individual to seek alternative social relationships through the Internet.
> (Hamburger and Ben-Artzi 2003: 76–77)

Through structural equation modelling these researchers demonstrated that it is the second explanation which is supported. Hence, neurotic women tend to be lonelier and are more likely to use social Internet services.

Others have found that, in particular, lonely adolescents enjoy making friends online. In a study by Gross *et al.* (2002) 130 young adolescents' well-being and online social interactions were examined. These researchers found that their participants opted to communicate mostly in private settings such as e-mail and Instant Messenger (IM) with friends they already knew offline. The types of topics they discussed were in the main ordinary intimate topics such as friends and gossip. Interestingly, the study found that young teens who reported feeling lonely or socially anxious at school on a daily basis were more likely to communicate through IM with people not well known to them (e.g. strangers). Gross *et al.* suggest that such individuals are using the Internet to avoid feeling alone. There are a number of questions still left unanswered from this study. For instance, do the adolescents who choose to find more companionship online feel less lonely and socially anxious as a consequence? Moreover, one space online that was not investigated in this study (most likely due to when the data were collected) was social networking sites.

Wolak *et al.*'s (2003) study confirms some of the results obtained by Gross *et al.* (2002). They were interested in whether most adolescents formed close friendships and romances online. Moreover, they were interested in how often young people encounter unwanted communication and sexual solicitations online. Similar to Gross *et al.*, they found that those adolescents with problems were more likely to develop close online relationships with other youths. This was especially the case for those who felt alienated from their parents. Unfortunately, these researchers did not assess whether these online relationships were a helpful alternative to offline relationships. So we are still left unconvinced as to whether forming online friendships when adolescents are experiencing rocky times is helpful or unhelpful.

Whitty and McLaughlin (2007) also contend that it is important to consider different spaces online when it comes to examining loneliness and Internet usage. They surveyed 150 undergraduate students from the UK about how they used the Internet for entertainment and also obtained scores for loneliness and Internet self-efficacy. The factor analysis they performed revealed three facets of online recreation, including using the Internet for: computer-based entertainment; to facilitate offline entertainment; and for information about the entertainment world. The participants in their study who scored higher on loneliness were more likely to use the Internet for computer-based entertainment (e.g. chat, downloading films and music). Whitty and McLaughlin suggested that the Internet represents a safe, low-risk social environment for lonely people. They believe that these activities could potentially be substitutes for engaging in FtF interactions. They also found that the lonely people in their sample were more likely to use the Internet to obtain information about the entertainment world. Whitty and McLaughlin argue that this result suggests that lonelier individuals are attracted to the Internet for entertainment as an alternative to offline entertainment. In addition, these researchers found that self-efficacy played an important role in determining if an individual was more likely to use some types of online entertainment. Individuals higher in Internet self-efficacy were more likely to use the Internet for computer-based entertainment and to facilitate offline entertainment. Whitty and McLaughlin suggest that an implication of such a finding is that if researchers find that use of the Internet for entertainment is beneficial for lonely people, then one might want to train lonely individuals to use the Internet more effectively.

Are we all talking to strangers?

Much of the research described above assumes that online communication is carried out between individuals unknown to one another offline. Of course this is not always the case. On a daily basis individuals e-mail and text work colleagues and offline friends and family and chat to them via IM. Some researchers have begun to consider the link between well-being and the different types of relationships one has online. For example, the study conducted by Gross *et al.* (2002) mentioned above found that young teens who reported feeling lonely or socially anxious at school were more likely to communicate through IM with people they did not know well (i.e. strangers). With the increase in popularity of social networking sites, especially where teens are concerned, it is imperative that we begin to learn more about the types of cyber-friends people are forming and whether they have close ties to these same individuals offline.

Online support groups

In addition to forming friendships online, individuals can seek out more formalised types of social support. Online support groups, for instance, have been set up by health professionals to assist individuals in distress. These sites provide both informational and emotional support, as well as a sense of a supportive community. The Pew Internet and American Life Project (2005) reports that eight out of ten American Internet users (79 per cent) used the Internet 'to find out about health information, ranging from information about a specific illness or disease to alternative treatments and advice on quitting smoking'. Moreover, 'research suggests that tens of millions of Americans use the Internet for psychoeducation, self-help, and support and that this number far exceeds those who would use the Internet for one-on-one counselling' (Chang 2005: 1). Given the number of lonely, socially anxious and depressed individuals who are flocking to the Internet, it is not surprising that the Internet abounds with social support groups. This has led psychologists to query the utility of online social support groups. Do they provide adequate, helpful and accurate information? Do they alleviate loneliness, social anxiety and depression? Or do they simply provide a place for the depressed, socially anxious and lonely to ruminate about their problems?

Online support might exist as bulletin boards, discussion boards or listservs, which are available 24 hours a day for individuals to leave messages or ask questions of the users of the board (see Eysenbach *et al.* 2004 for a review). It exists as web pages, sometimes constructed by experts, while others are designed by laypeople. They can also exist as chat rooms, some of which are moderated. Online support is typically specialised, ranging from psychological problems (such as support groups for anorexics, the depressed, individuals contemplating suicide and people with particular phobias) to disabilities to physical ailments (e.g. specific forms of cancer or for individuals with sexually transmitted diseases). Online support groups can be autonomous self-help groups or led by mental health professionals.

What kind of support?

Some researchers have lurked on online support discussion boards to analyse the content of their pages. Overall it would seem that messages in these groups are either informative or supportive. For example, Braithwaite *et al.* (1999) examined a disabilities social support group. They analysed 1472 social support postings from 42 members. Drawing from Cutrona and Suhr's (1992) categories – information support, tangible assistance, esteem support, network support and emotional support (interrater reliability of .76 from two scorers was obtained) – it was revealed that the most common form of support was emotional (40 per cent). Finn (1999) analysed an online self-help group that also focused on disability issues. This time 718 messages were analysed from 42 users (interrater reliability of .82 from two scorers was obtained). They found that most common categories included: providing support and empathy (21.2 per cent); providing information (15.3 per cent); being devoted to problem solving (14.4 per cent); and involving expressions of feelings or catharsis (12.3 per cent). Sharf (1997) analysed messages posted by 825 participants to a listserv (a space online similar to a discussion board that individuals need to subscribe to in order to receive messages). Similar to the other studies on online social support she identi- fied three main categories of messages: information; social support; and personal information. Similarly, Winzelberg (1997) examined an online support group for individuals with eating disorders. Three hundred and six messages were coded by two raters, who identified four categories: search- ing for meaning; adjusting to changes; providing support and encour- agement; and sharing experiences narratively. Winzelberg argued that members of this group used similar helping strategies to those found in FtF groups. In the main, the members provided emotional support, information and feedback.

Some studies have tried to make distinctions between similar types of support groups. Blank and Adams-Blodnieks (2007) focused their research on two cancer groups – breast and prostate – and examined the content of their asynchronous bulletin boards. They chose these two cancers as one would expect them to be gendered, with obviously more men accessing the prostate cancer online support group and more women accessing the breast cancer online support group. They did, however, find some differences between the groups in the senders of the messages. For the breast cancer group, 87 per cent of the messages were from breast cancer survivors, 3 per cent from spouses, and 9 per cent from family or friends. For the prostate cancer group, only 54 per cent of the messages were from prostate cancer survivors, 29 per cent from spouses, and 17 per cent from family and friends. From their analysis of 492 postings, four main categories emerged: support; medical/treatment; emotional expression; and intimacy/sexuality. When considering the two groups the proportions of messages dedicated to each of these topics differed significantly. For the breast cancer group the proportion of postings dedicated to each category included: support (45.5 per cent); medical/treatment (28.9 per cent); emotional expression (22.8 per cent); intimacy/sexuality (2.2 per cent). For the prostate cancer group the proportion of postings dedicated to each category included: medical/ treatment (43.2 per cent); support (36.1 per cent); emotional expression (12.3 per cent); intimacy/sexuality (8.4 per cent). It is noteworthy that the breast cancer group were more likely to focus on support, whereas the prostate cancer group were more likely to focus on information.

Preece and Ghozati (2001) have also found that sites which were female in nature had higher percentages of empathic messages than sites more oriented towards men. Blank and Adams-Blodnieks (2007) highlight the importance of considering who is sending the messages to these groups. For instance, for the prostate cancer group, a larger proportion of wives were communicating than were their spouses on the breast cancer group. Blank and Adams-Blodnieks contend:

> This may indicate that traditional gender roles are being played out – women as 'caretakers' may feel more comfortable seeking help for or feel responsible for their family's well being. Men, on the other hand, seem more comfortable asking about their own issues but not to delve into a group about breast cancer to seek information or discuss reactions.

Problems with online support groups

Some of the negative consequences of online support groups include: misinformation; conflict among group members; and possible development of Internet addiction (Mallen *et al.* 2005). Mallen and Vogel (2005) suggest that such groups be treated with caution as they are not the same as therapy. They contend that obtaining misinformation could be more damaging to an individual than no information at all. Incorrect information might be written on the groups' websites or could be voluntarily given by its members. Despite good intentions, not all information placed on such sites is correct. As Sillence *et al.* (2007) have found in respect to health sites, individuals do not always make the correct decisions about which websites they can trust.

Arguably, however, professionals can prevent some of these negative outcomes (Mallen *et al.* 2005). Chang (2005) has suggested that universities' counselling centres ought to be more proactive in developing psychoeducational resources online. Mallen and Vogel (2005) believe that counselling services should not stop there. Instead of just providing psychoeducation and self-help, these web pages should be a gateway for students to seek FtF services.

Overcoming the obstacles

Some online support groups draw from professionals and lay people. Hsiung (2000), also known as Dr Bob, for instance, runs an online self-help group named the Psycho-Babble group, which he argues draws from the best of both worlds. This support group runs as an asynchronous message board which people subscribe to as members for free. In this online support group, 'the mental health professional focuses on maintaining the supportive milieu and the members of the group focus on providing the support for each other' (Hsiung 2000: 935). Conflict is avoided by monitoring and comments to the board by Hsiung:

> When posters are considered by the author not to have been civil, messages to that effect are posted. Others would do this privately, by email, and that would have the advantage of being less embarrassing. If done with sensitivity, however, posting offers the advantages of clarifying the limits for others, modelling conflict resolution, diminishing any paranoia about activity 'behind the scenes,' and allowing others to contribute to the process.
>
> (Hsiung 2000: 938)

Members who continue uncivil communication are blocked from sending any further postings, but are permitted to continue to read others' postings. The monitor of the group has other controls. Names of the posters are either deleted or replaced by letters and some messages are edited if they are too long. It is rare for incorrect information to be posted, and when it does this is typically corrected by another member (Hsiung 2000). On some occasions, however, it is necessary for Hsiung to make a correction.

Hsiung (2000) does admit though that not all the problems associated with online support groups are obviated by having professionals involved. Some group members have admitted that they feel addicted to the group, with one member posting on average 6.8 messages per day. A further problem described by Hsiung is that he is unable to prevent members from assuming 'multiple identities'. He suggests that some members might do this to 'simulate more support for particular sides of issues or to rejoin the group after being blocked' (Hsiung 2000: 947).

Crisis situation support groups

Dr Bob is a good example of a fairly successful general online support group. However, many online support groups focus on particular problems.

Barak (2007) has described an Israeli project named SAHAR, which is a non-profit group that was set up to attract people in a crisis situation. As Barak describes:

> The idea behind SAHAR, then, was to initiate a virtual, psycho-logically enhanced location that would attract people in a crisis situation and offer them a virtual listening ear, a safe virtual shoulder to lean on, and a warm virtual hug by anonymous, skilled helpers, all the while assuring such users anonymity and confidentiality. When necessary, furthermore, it would also organize a rescue operation to save a person's life.
>
> (p. 973)

This website is accessed more than 350 times per day. Barak (2007) claims that SAHAR has participated, on numerous occasions, in rescue operations of individuals who were attempting or threatening to commit suicide. This service is also free, and like Dr Bob's support group is based on clear psychological foundations. SAHAR offers information and support. The information online is updated, detailed and relates to any area of distress (Barak 2007). The site links to the offline world by providing a reading list of books and articles for those who prefer to read offline. It allows for working with groups, while ensuring that all participants are anonymous. Unlike telephone support, the site gives both synchronous and asynchronous support. It also has experienced counsellors for the site and provides detailed information on telephone hotlines and emergency services (it recognises that some people might prefer offline forms of communication such as the telephone).

SAHAR tries to provide a variety of modes of online communication (given that not everyone prefers one form over another). Individuals can communicate synchronously (through chat or ICQ – whichever they prefer) with trained anonymous helpers. This live service operates three hours every night (due to practical reasons – requiring staff to run it). Nonetheless, for emergency referrals a helper is available at most times and will respond fairly rapidly to a person in crisis. Asynchronous communication, in the form of e-mail, is available to those who prefer this mode of communication. A web form is available for those who wish to remain anonymous – given that e-mail can reveal someone's identity.

A measure of the site's success are the reports obtained by cooperating authorities (e.g. police) who have said that SAHAR contributed directly to saving the life of someone 'during an advanced stage of the suicide attempt' (Barak 2007). So far one hundred such occasions have been reported by authorities. Individuals have written to the site expressing their gratitude. Empirical evidence has also been collected to verify the success of the site (e.g. Barak and Miron 2005). Like Hsiung (2000), Barak (2007) admits that the site is not perfect. For instance, sometimes there are fake messages and possibly there is the online version of 'Munchausen by proxy syndrome'. Others, Barak argues, might be acting out. Even if the percentage of these individuals is small (approximately 5 per cent) it can still drain the helpers, accelerating burn-out.

Dynamics of online support

Some researchers have questioned whether the degree of active involvement in using an online support group affects the distress levels of those who use them (Barak and Dolev-Cohen 2006). Drawing from participants of the SAHAR site described above, Barak and Dolev-Cohen (2006) randomly selected 20 adolescents (15 girls and 5 boys) to examine this question. Three months' worth of messages that these participants had written on the site were analysed and compared as to how they differed over time. They found that the more involved an individual was in the group (involvement being measured as number of postings they wrote, responding to others and receiving replies to their own messages), the more likely their distress levels were to decrease over time. The main implication of this study, according to Barak and Dolev-Cohen, was that:

> Appropriate instructions should be delivered to participants in order to encourage their active involvement in the group, which will conse-quently promote their emotional relief. Likewise, online support-group facilitators should be instructed and trained accordingly and, they should also play a major role in encouraging participants' active involvement.
>
> (p. 189)

Conclusions

Overall it would seem that 'real' online support is available for people. Mallen *et al.* (2005) claim that the research which has investigated the use of online support groups has typically found benefits for participants of these groups (but see Eysenbach *et al.* 2004 who report no positive or negative effect). It would seem from the general overview presented here that online support groups do have much to offer. The few empirical studies available on the success of these groups suggest that if professionals are also involved in the mechanisms of the group the online support group has a great deal to offer individuals in psychological need.

5   Online research, ethics and the candid participant

The Internet is increasingly becoming a space that researchers are viewing not only as an object of research, but also as a tool for conducting research itself. Online, researchers can administer surveys, collect text and images and carry out interviews. The Internet provides researchers with a more readily accessible pool of individuals to study. It also provides easier access to a large number of participants, where one can collect worldwide samples. Researchers can have access to samples that are often more difficult to reach (e.g. the elderly, people with disabilities, people in prison and hospital). Moreover, we are privy to more fringe or deviant sexual activities that are not so easily observable offline. In addition, researchers have text readily available to use from e-mails, chat records, discussion boards, and so forth. As Mann and Stewart (2000) rightly claim, the Internet, it would seem, is an ideal place to recruit individuals.

Despite the opportunities that the Internet provides for researchers to observe and collect broad and interesting samples, social scientists need to proceed with caution. As this chapter will discuss, in addition to old ethical issues raised in respect to offline research, conducting research online raises new ethical issues.

Online research and the candid participant

As noted in Chapter 2, there is considerable evidence that people's responses to online surveys are often more open and candid, compared to paper or FtF interviews. Back in 1996, Weisband and Kiesler conducted a meta-analysis of interviews and surveys conducted FtF or via a computer. Looking at the results of 39 studies completed between 1969 and 1994, they concluded that administering research via a computer significantly increases self-disclosure. Importantly, this effect was present whether or not it was an interview situation or pencil and paper tests, although the effect was twice as strong for interviews. This suggests that reducing social cues or presence of the researcher in an interview context, a side effect of computerisation, has a beneficial impact on respondents' self-disclosure. Weisband and Kiesler also looked at the impact of the question type on this effect, and found that the effect of using a computer was stronger when the questions were sensitive, personal or risky, and when the population being sampled was vulnerable (e.g. prisoners and patients).

Although Weisband and Kiesler (1996) found some evidence that the impact of computers on self-disclosure was declining over time, there is a considerable amount of more recent evidence to suggest that completion of research measures via computer increases self-disclosure. For instance, Joinson (1999) randomly allocated students to a web or pencil and paper condition, whereupon they completed a measure of social desirability. The results showed a significant effect of media – the students answering via the web form scored higher on the social desirability measure, signifying more candid responses. Tourangeau (2004; see also Chapter 2) reviews a large number of studies that suggest people are more likely to admit to socially undesirable behaviours, or to disclose sensitive information about themselves, to a computer compared to FtF or via pencil and paper.

Designing for candour

Researchers need to be aware that this increased self-disclosure and truthfulness in online research environments is not guaranteed. The greater sophistication of online research, as well as people's experience of using such tools, threatens to remove the advantages outlined above. However, a number of techniques are available to encourage candid disclosure, or conversely to increase secrecy if reversed.

Privacy

Of course, anyone who has undertaken research involving people knows how important it is to stress the anonymity and confidentiality of responses. On the Internet, such reassurances are just as important, if not more so because of the possibilities for compromising confidentiality. For instance, Joinson *et al.* (2007) report that techniques to improve response rates, such as personalised salutations in e-mail invites, can reduce people's perceived privacy and their willingness to disclose sensitive information. Moon (1998) found that increasing the geographic distance between participant and server led to higher levels of self-disclosure, presumably because the larger distance reduced the potential vulnerability of the participant. The inclusion of a strong privacy policy may also have an effect on participants' willingness to disclose personal information. Joinson *et al.* (in press) reported that people disclosed more information to a sign-up page when it was preceded by a strong privacy policy, rather than information about the research project.

Trustworthiness

As will be discussed later in this volume, trust has a number of dimensions, including the competence, reputation and intentions (benevolent or

Mazilla Firefox

http://www.survance.net/

Getting Started Latest Headlines Virgin Wines Wine BBC Santino gm b2 Google Affdwrb bti imb.net Welcome to SilkyMail Apple News Amazon Microsoft Outlook W...

Personality, Openness and Life Experiences logo!!!

The information that you choose to provide during this survey will be collected and stored by the researchers at the Open University, a large higher education institution in the United Kingdom. Backup copies of the datafile will be kept off-site on portable media (memory sticks and CD-ROM). We may also pass your information on to our collaborators for further analysis.

You can choose not to provide information to any item, and you are free to withdraw from the survey at any stage by simply closing the window.

While we will do all we can to protect your privacy, you should be aware that your responses could be intercepted by third parties such as hackers or law enforcement agencies.

Your browser may also store data locally in your computer's hard drive, with the result that other people using your computer could potentially find it. The data you submit may also be held in a temporary store or cache maintained by your university, internet service provider or employer.

Web-servers automatically collect i.p. numbers for each person who visits a page. These numbers are the 'Internet address' of the computer you are using. We use the i.p. numbers associated with each response to check for people completing the survey more than once.

If you are happy to continue please click below to go to the final page of the survey. If you have any questions, please e-mail us using this address.

BEGIN THE STUDY

Figure 5.1 Untrustworthy, low privacy research website (from Joinson *et al.* in press)

malevolent) of the research organisation. People's initial interpretation of the trustworthiness of a website tends to be made very quickly using design-based heuristics (Sillence *et al.* 2006), including an inappropriate name for the website, a messy layout and the inclusion of adverts (Sillence *et al.* 2006). Joinson *et al.* (in press) compared self-disclosure to a trustworthy and untrustworthy research site. The untrustworthy site was hosted on a fake domain (www.surveylance.net) and included adverts, spelling mistakes and HMTL coding errors (see Figure 5.1). The trustworthy site had an educational URL, no adverts, no mistakes and no coding errors. Perhaps not surprisingly, self-disclosure was significantly higher to the trustworthy questionnaire, especially when the privacy statement was weak (as shown in Figure 5.1).

Of course, most university-based research has in-built high trust based on the organisational affiliation of the researchers. But as increasing numbers of social scientists turn to third-party online survey companies (e.g. survey-monkey) to host their surveys, so issues of establishing trustworthiness will come to the fore.

Reciprocity

Self-disclosure tends to be reciprocated (Archer 1976): that is, within an interaction, one person's intimacies tend to be reciprocated in terms of level and type by the communication partner. Violation of this rule can lead to discomfort and withdrawal from an interaction. To test the notion that people respond to computers as social actors, Moon (2000) tested self-disclosure reciprocity in the collection of data via stand-alone computers. She found that when the computer essentially disclosed information about itself (e.g. 'Sometimes this computer is used by people who don't know how to operate it. It ends up crashing. What are some of the things that make you furious?'), the participants reciprocated in kind, leading to a greater breadth and depth of disclosure. In a pilot study testing the applicability of this effect to web-based surveys, Joinson (2001) assigned participants to either an experimenter disclosing or non-disclosing condition. In the experimenter disclosing condition participants were directed to a web page with information about the experimenter, while in the non-disclosing condition participants did not receive information about the experimenter until after the experimental procedure. All participants answered six personal questions using free text. Although in the study there was no effect of reciprocal self-disclosure on the depth of self-disclosure, there was an effect on the breadth of disclosure. That is, participants who answered the questions following self-disclosure by the experimenter went on to disclose more about themselves, but not with any greater intimacy, than those who went straight to the questions.

It should also be noted that people will not only reciprocate disclosure, but they will also tend to mimic conversational structure (Niederhoffer and Pennebaker 2002) – not only in content, but also length. So, it might be possible for researchers to encourage certain types of response through the text they use.

Control and impression management

Socially desirable responding may well contain two distinct aspects: impression formation and self-deception (Paulhus 1984). Theoretically, anonymity will reduce socially desirable responding based on the desire to impression manage (Paulhus 1984), but it will not influence participants' self-deception. Empirical results, however, are mixed. In some cases anonymity has reduced only the impression formation aspect of socially desirable responding (Paulhus 1984), while in others both aspects have been reduced through anonymity (Booth-Kewley *et al.* 1992). Fox and Schwartz (2002) found that by increasing participants' control during the research process, the impression management aspect of socially desirable responding was also increased. Control was introduced into the procedure by allowing participants' choice as to the type of questions they wanted to answer, allowing movement through the questions to change or check responses and providing sample questions to inform their choice. Participants given increased control also rated the test more positively than those with no control. They had more trust in the research, were less anxious and said that they were likely to respond with more candour (even though this was not found when experimentally tested). In the condition with weakened control – where participants were given a short time to answer each question, and could not move back to previous items – impression management was reduced. Fox and Schwartz (2002) found no effect of anonymity, although this may be due to their particular sample (people undergoing selection for an elite military group).

For CMC-based interviews and focus groups, the same principle will apply. According to Walther (1996), asynchronous CMC has substantial impression management advantages over synchronous CMC – people have the time to edit and check their messages before sending. Moreover, the time afforded by asynchronous CMC should also reduce the cognitive load associated with the need to combine answering a question with impression management. While these are desirable qualities for the building of an online relationship and affiliation, they do not sit easily with a researcher's desire to elicit candid responses. It would be expected then that synchronous CMC methods should reduce impression management, and at least in theory should provide better quality data, particularly when dealing with sensitive topics.

Ethical guidelines offline and how these should also be applied online

There are a number of ethical considerations that researchers are expected to adhere to when conducting their offline research that can also be applied online. Some of these practical considerations include: informed consent, withdrawal of consent, confidentiality and debriefing.

Informed consent requires researchers to be up front, from the beginning, about the aims of their research and how they are going to utilise the data. In offline research individuals are typically given an information sheet about the study and sign a form to give their consent. However, this is not always achievable online. One way around this is to set up a web page that provides participants with information about the study together with contact details of the researchers involved. Giving consent might be achieved in a number of ways. A website might be set up where once the survey or interview has been conducted participants can click a button to indicate that they are willing for the researcher to use their data in their study. In some countries written consent is required. In such cases, the researcher could provide the participant with a form to download and sign and either fax or send to the research via postal mail.

Some spaces (e.g. chat rooms, newsgroups and bulletin boards) on the web are moderated. When online spaces are moderated, it is probably appropriate to contact the moderators first to ask their permission to target individuals interacting within this space. This is akin to contacting an organisation prior to targeting individuals within that organisation. Wysocki's (1998) research on adult bulletin boards is a good example of how one might go about contacting moderators of an online site. In this study, Wysocki was upfront with her identity as a researcher. She originally approached the systems operators and told them that she was a sociologist who was interested in using Pleasure Pit to collect data. The operators were enthusiastic about her research and she was invited to meet them and learn how the bulletin board service operated. From there the moderators placed a notice on their site informing users of the site about Wysocki's study.

As with offline research, we need also to consider up until what point a participant can withdraw consent. The end point of withdrawal of consent might be, for instance, after the submission of the online survey, or at the conclusion of the online interview the interviewer might find confirmation that the participant is happy to allow the researcher to include the transcript in the study. These are issues unique to online research in respect to withdrawal of consent. For example, the computer could crash midway through an interview or survey. Consequently, mechanisms need to be put into place to allow that participant to rejoin the research if desired, and consent should not be assumed if it is not certain why the interview ceased. Additionally, in circumstances such as the computer or server crashing, researchers should have a system to enable debriefing, especially if the research is asking questions of a personal nature. This might be achieved by providing a contact e-mail or phone number prior to the commencement of the study. Moreover, as Nosek *et al.* (2002) suggest, debriefing can be made available by providing a 'leave the study' button on each page of an online survey, which would allow individuals to abort the study but still be directed to a debriefing page. These researchers also suggest that it might be a good idea for participants to be given a list of FAQs.

Confidentiality is another concern for researchers. As with offline research, if researchers wish to represent their participants in the write-up of qualitative data (e.g. interviews) they might elect to use pseudonyms. A unique aspect of the Internet is that individuals often represent themselves online using a 'screen name', rather than their real name. When interviewing people online, interviewers might only be privy to the participants' screen name. However, when presenting these people's narratives should the research be allowed to use these screen names in the transcripts they published? The answer is most likely no. This is because online people might still be identified by others, which does not allow them to be completely anonymous in the write-up of their story. The same might be said of online communities – to name a particular chat room, bulletin board or newsgroup might break confidentiality. For this reason, it is usually not a good idea to use quotes verbatim in research – it is simple to search for a quote and find the author using a search engine.

Private versus public spaces

The boundaries between what constitutes a public and private space online are often fuzzy. For example, a chat room is a public space. However, those interacting within this space might perceive this as a more private space. Hence, as we have discussed earlier in this chapter, individuals might feel less inhibited and more likely to disclose personal details about themselves in this space that they might not typically do in FtF settings. Is it ethical for researchers to lurk in these spaces without announcing their presence or declaring they are in the space as researchers collecting data? Is it ethically justifiable for researchers to lurk online and download material without the knowledge or consent of the individuals involved? Importantly, communication might have occurred originally in what was considered a private space (e.g. a newsgroup), which subsequently became a public space (as happened with newsgroups through web archiving).

Ferri (1999, cited in Mann and Stewart 2000: 46) asks the question 'Who is the intended audience of an electronic communication – and does it include you as a researcher?' How intrusive a method is lurking? Researchers need seriously to question whether it is ethical to lurk in spaces online without seeking permission from their participants. They also need to consider how examining a group for research might affect the fabric of the group they are studying. One way to go about this is to first ask permission from the group whether they are permitted to use their conversations as data in their research. An alternative approach might be to ask for permission after collecting data. Not all researchers agree that the right to investigate individuals online is clear-cut. Bruckman (2002) has stated:

> If we are too lax in our ethics, we risk violating the rights of individual subjects and disrupting communities we study . . . On the other hand, if we are too strict we may hamper our ability to understand the medium.
>
> (p. 218)

Walther (2002) has stated:

> While some participants have an expectation of privacy it is extremely misplaced. More fruitful efforts might be made in educating the public about the vulnerability of Internet postings to scrutiny – an inherent aspect of many Internet venues – than by debating whether or not such scrutiny should be sanctioned in research.
>
> (p. 207)

He adds: 'Researchers must make their own individual ethical decisions with regard to activities such as quoting or reflecting names or pseudonyms in their ultimate publications' (p. 208).

However, not all authors agree (e.g. Ess 2007). Moreover, some have found evidence that individuals do not enjoy having some information they place online used for research purposes. For example, it has been found that teenagers in particular feel quite negatively about having their profiles studied in research and they do not feel comfortable about researchers lurking on sites to study them (Hudson and Bruckman 2004; Walther *et al.* 2008). It is important to note that the recent British Psychological Society's guidance for online research cautions that privacy should be the default assumption, rather than an afterthought. This may be particularly so for subgroups of Internet users such as gamblers or those seeking support online.

Online deception

According to the Australian National Health and Medical Research Council (which set the ethical guidelines for Australian research):

> As a general principle, deception of, concealment of the purposes of a study from, or covert observation of, identifiable participants are not considered ethical because they are contrary to the principle of respect for persons in that free and fully informed consent cannot be given.
>
> (NHMRC 1999)

However, they do state that under certain unusual circumstances deception is unavoidable when there is no alternative method to conduct one's research. However, in these circumstances individuals must be given the opportunity to withdraw data obtained from them during the research that they did not originally give consent to. Moreover, the council stipulates that 'such activities will not corrupt the relationship between researchers and research in general with the community at large' (NHMRC 1999).

While many studies have followed such guidelines, there are others who have not. Lamb's (1998) research, for example, could be described as a highly deceptive study, which did not entirely respect the rights of the participants (see Whitty 2004a). Lamb (1998) examined others in chat rooms by participating himself in a chat room. He mostly visited sites for adults seeking young men and in his interactions with his unsuspecting participants he adopted several identities, all of which were teenage bisexual males. In about half of the occasions he chatted in a public chat room Lamb was invited into a private room where the researcher and the unknowing participant engaged mostly in sexual conversations. Lamb's ultimate goal was to determine whether deviancy is evident in chat rooms, the implication being that this is a place for paedophiles to abuse children. While this research is arguably attempting to explore an important issue, did Lamb go about his research in an ethical manner? Participants were deceived throughout the research. While there were hints given to each participant that this might be recorded and later utilised in research, the intention behind the interactions was more covert than overt. In addition, Lamb (1998) does not state that he provided an opportunity for participants to withdraw data obtained from them during the research. While some have questioned whether lurking is an ethical way to collect data, Lamb's (1998) research could be said to have crossed this line when he decided not to simply observe but also to participate (Whitty 2004a).

Whitty (2004a) recalls that at a conference she attended there was debate as to whether it was necessary to disclose one's true identity as a researcher in cyberspace. One academic stated that given that everyone lies in cyberspace, lying was the norm and hence expected. This academic concluded that therefore it was permissible for researchers not to reveal all their cards, given that this is already a deceptive environment. This might be somewhat supported. However, as Whitty (2004a) asks, does this give researchers the right to be deceptive?

Conclusions

As an object and tool of research the Internet has revolutionised many social science inquiries. However, it is important that researchers are aware not only of the ethical issues involved in online research, but also the potential interaction between how people behave online, the design of their study and the eventual results. There is remarkably little research that considers the impact of medium on the research process – despite many years of, say, CMC research being particularly informative for online interviewing.

6 Online deception, fraud, spam and cons

> To recognize untruth as a condition of life: that, to be sure, means to resist customary value-sentiments in a dangerous fashion and a philosophy which ventures to do so places itself, by the act alone, beyond good and evil.
>
> (Nietzsche 2003: 36)

As we have noted in earlier chapters, the freedom offered by the Internet truthfully to disclose information about oneself paradoxically also allows us to engage in creative self-presentation, misrepresentation and outright lies. Cases of deception online hold a morbid fascination for researchers and Internet users alike. The case of Alex and Joan (reported by Van Gelder 1991) is often cited as a classic case of identity deception. In this case Alex created a persona (called 'Joan') who became a confidante of many of the women on a discussion board, some of whom Alex had sexual relations with. Joan avoided FtF meetings by disclosing that she was disabled. Of course, Joan was Alex, which caused considerable outrage in the community. A number of other cases are reasonably well documented. For instance, 'Nowheremom' (a female created by a male online community member, whom he subsequently dated and then killed off in a car accident) has been outlined by Joinson (2003) and Joinson and Dietz-Uhler (2002). Feldman (2000) further describes four cases where people claimed serious illness on support communities, only to be unmasked as fakes later (he calls this 'Munchausen by Internet'). In this chapter, we examine the nature of deception, its prevalence online, the impact lying has on those lied to and how to identify a deceiver online.

What is deception?

Lying, after all, is suggestive of game theory. It involves at least two people, a liar and someone who is lied to; it transmits information, the credibility and veracity of which are important; it influences some choice another is to make that the liar anticipates; the choice to lie or not to lie is part of the liar's choice of strategy; and the possibility of a lie presumably occurs to the second party, and may be judged against some *a priori* expectations; and the payoff configurations are rich in their possibilities, since a lie can be told for the good of the victim, the truth can be told to pave the way for a later lie, and a lie can even be told with the intention that it not be believed.

(Schelling 1968: 35)

Buller and Burgoon (1996) define deception as 'a message knowingly transmitted by a sender to foster a false belief or conclusion by the receiver' (p. 205). Similarly, Bok (1989) has defined a lie as 'any intentionally deceptive message which is *stated*. Such statements are most often made verbally or in writing, but can of course also be conveyed via smoke signals, Morse code, sign language, and the like' (p. 13). Hancock (2007: 290) defines digital deception as, 'the intentional control of information in a technologically mediated message to create a false belief in the receiver of the message'.

Each of the above definitions shares a number of characteristics: something is deception only if it is intentional – otherwise it is a mistake or misunderstanding; and there must be intent to create false belief, which disqualifies deception intended to amuse (e.g. irony). Hancock (2007) adds that digital deception must also be enacted using information communication technology.

The type of deception opportunities available online are constantly changing as technology develops. For instance, it is not common to reprogramme GPS systems to provide a false location to a spouse when she or he requests it, simply because such technology is not commonplace. However, if tracking by mobile phone becomes a popular service in the future, you can bet there will be people deceiving each other using it.

Types of online deception

DePaulo *et al.* (1996) have argued that lying is a part of daily life. The Internet has simply provided a new place for individuals to lie. Of concern to researchers have been the types of lies evident in cyberspace, and whether people are more inclined to lie on the Internet compared to FtF or the telephone. Donath (1998) identifies a number of different types of Internet deception, including false e-mail addresses and signatures, category deception (i.e. pretending to be a different gender), trolling (posting deliberately confrontational messages) and identity concealment (withholding information, rather than providing misleading information).

Hancock (2007) divides digital deception into identity-based (deception based on creating a false identity or affiliation) and message-based (deception based within the content of a communication between two or more people). In keeping with Hancock's typology, we will consider identity-based and message-based digital deception separately.

Table 6.1 Percentages of what people lie about in chat rooms (adapted from Whitty 2002)

Item	Men	Women	17–20 yrs	21–55 yrs
Lied age	63	60	66	53
Lied gender	28	18	23	22
Lied occupation	56	42	50	47
Lied education	40	25	31	35
Lied income	44	28	35	37

Identity-based deception

As the examples given at the beginning of this chapter illustrate, online it is possible to be whatever you might wish – a different gender, age, nationality or even a sufferer of a chronic disease – regardless of whether or not it has any basis in reality. Donath (1998) includes not only category deception within this grouping, but also trolling, where a person pretends to be a legitimate member of a group or community, while truly being motivated by a desire to cause argument and confusion.

Whitty (2002a) found in her investigation of 320 chat rooms that men and women admitted to lying in chat rooms about their age, gender, occupation, education and income (see Table 6.1). Men were significantly more likely than women to lie about gender, occupation, education and income. Younger people (aged 17–20 years) were more likely than older people (aged 21–55 years) to lie about their age. Although identity-based deception in computer mediated communication garners much attention, it is the financially motivated forms of deception (e.g. fraud) that impose a real cost on Internet users. In the following section, we look at the use of deception in scams and fraud online.

419 'Nigerian e-mail' scam

I am writing you this mail from my father's home at . . . London believing that you will be of tremendous help in my effort to save the last of my family legacy. I choose to reach you through this medium because it is the fastest and most reliable way of communication, as I wish to solicit for your unflinching support and cooperation.

My name is Mr. West Alamieyeseigha, the heir to the Alamieyeseigha's family. My family's ordeal started sometime last year when my father, then the Governor of Bayelsa state in Southern Nigeria was at loggerhead with the Federal Government following his campaign against the insensitivity of the government to the plight of the Niger delta region, the region that produces the country crude oil – the major foreign exchange earner of my country.

Shortly before his arrest in London UK, my father had series of meeting with the federal authorities part of which was aimed at getting him drop his campaign for true federalism and resource control but he turned down all the juicy promises that was offered him hence the plan to get him set up. He was arrested and detained in London last year. Somewhere along the line, he escaped to his State Bayelsa but not without the collaboration of the UK authorities who claimed he jumped bail. My ill mother of 50, Mrs. Margaret Alamieyeseigha was also humiliated in London and charged for money laundry offences.

I am certain you know much about this case however, you can make further enquiries. However, my reason for contacting you is to solicit your support and collaboration in securing my family legacy. I am contacting you on the instructions of my mother who asked me to seek for a reliable foreigner who will help us invest some of the undetected fund belonging to my father kept in private safes worth over $20,000,000.00. I shall provide you with details of how to access the money if you provide me with investment information in your country. For this Information and your collaboration, 30 per cent of the entire money will be your reward for your assistance.

I shall detail you further when you indicate interest to help us. Meanwhile you may reach me on . . .

This e-mail is what is known as the 'Nigerian scam', of which there are many versions (in Chapter 7 we describe another version known as the 'romance scam'). It is also known as the 'advance fee fraud' or the '419 scam' (so named because of the Section number of Nigerian criminal law that applies to it). It actually began as postal mail and since the advent of the Internet these scammers took advantage of free e-mail and mailing lists to target many more potential victims. In most cases the mail appears to be sent from an African country and/or an individual who is typically Nigerian, although others are sent from different African countries and in recent years from Asia and eastern European countries. All these forms of e-mail refer to a large amount of funds that is trapped or frozen for a variety of reasons (e.g. unclaimed estate, corrupt executive, dying Samaritan). In each case they offer the recipient rich rewards for simply helping government officials or family members out of an embarrassing or legal problem. As illustrated in the e-mail, the recipient is offered over $6,000,000 for their assistance.

Those that respond to such an e-mail (and surprisingly there have been a number of people conned) then gradually experience problems with the financial transaction. Initially, the paperwork is said to be delayed and officials need to be bribed. The recipient is then asked to send money to bribe the officials. The money asked of them seems insignificant in light of the huge windfall they will ultimately gain. Delays continue and more financial support is asked of the recipient. It becomes more difficult for them to refuse given that they have already invested a significant amount of their own money into the deal. Once the recipient claims to have no more funds or begins to make threats, they never hear from the scammers again nor do they see any money.

A number of people across the globe have in fact been conned by this scam. One such case is reported in *The New Yorker* by Zuckoff (2006). He writes that in 2001 an American Christian psychotherapist named John Worley fell for the scam. Zuckoff reports that Worley seemed an unlikely victim given that he supposedly had a good understanding of people and their motives, so much so that he developed a psychological profiling tool which is meant to reveal an individual's unique desires and needs and could purportedly predict behavioural responses. Within minutes of receiving the e-mail Worley responded that he was interested in helping and seemed satisfied with the explanation that he had been identified by the South African Department of Home Affairs. Initially, he was required to pay upfront costs, such as a storage facility for the money. He was told that he would possibly be required to travel to South Africa to collect the money. He would receive almost a third of more than sixteen million US dollars. Worley then claimed that he could not finance the operation but was prepared to act as a middle man and curator of the funds. Following from this, as promised, he was sent a cheque for $47,500. When the suspicious Worley rang the bank it was sent from, he learned that it was a counterfeit cheque. However, this is not the end of the story.

Zuckoff claims that Worley's egotism lead to his downfall – as he always believed he had the upper hand in this situation. After the cheque proved to be false and a replacement was not sent, Worley attempted to end the partnership. However, a few days later he received an e-mail from another Nigerian who claimed to be the eldest surviving son of a late Nigerian general. He was told that the first contact had been acting on his behalf but had bungled so badly that he had been forced to step into the breach. This was then followed by an e-mail from someone who claimed to be the general's widow asking Worley for his help. Worley claimed later to be excited by being on the verge of becoming rich while simultaneously assisting a woman in distress. He then spent several thousand US dollars on an attorney who specialised in international tax planning. Worley dismissed the attorney's warnings against this apparent get-rich-quick opportunity. He then spent $4,300 opening an account in a Bermuda-based bank so that the money would not be traced back to the US and hence tax would not have to be paid. Next the scammers convinced Worley to wire more than $8,000 in order to retain a lawyer and to cover bank and late fees. The plot continues with the scammers delaying proceedings and then managing to convince Worley to allow them to file false documentation claiming he was a private aviation contractor. In addition, in a counselling session he managed to convince one of his clients also to join the scheme and part with their money. The scammers continued to convince Worley that more money was required on his behalf and provided reasons as to why the proceedings were being delayed.

In May 2005 Worley went on trial in the US District Court in Boston on charges of bank fraud, money laundering and possession of counterfeit cheques. He was found guilty on all counts and sentenced to two years in prison and a restitution of almost $600,000. When Zuckoff (2006) interviewed him a week later, Worley stated, 'The communications that I had with those people were so convincing that I really believed that they were real, they were true.'

In his article, Zuckoff also reports that a statement by the US State Department claims that '419' scams began to proliferate when there was a collapse in oil prices in the mid-1980s due to severe economic upheaval in Nigeria. The department states that some of the scammers have been known to be violent, often encouraging individuals to travel to Nigeria or other countries where they fall victim to kidnapping, extortion and in rare cases murder.

The obvious motivation for those who have been conned by this scam is greed. However, some people have been pulled in through appeals to their altruistic side (indeed, in some cases they have offered help with no financial reward for themselves). However, psychologically what is of interest is what leads some individuals to trust others who in hindsight seem clearly to be scammers. One explanation could simply be that because so few people are conned by such scams certain personality types are more likely to be conned. In the case mentioned above, Zuckoff notes that Worley had compulsive tendencies.

Other e-mail scams

The Nigerian scam is probably the most well-known e-mail scam. However, there are various other e-mail scams which try to con individuals into handing over money or giving out their bank account details. For example, there is the work at home and business opportunity scam (some of which invite individuals to invest in fake companies); the clairvoyant/psychic e-mail scam (a pseudo clairvoyant requests money for an intervention from the pseudo psychic to prevent bad luck); the fake job offer (which attempts to acquire personal information from the recipient or trick them into showing up for a multilevel marketing pitch); and the fake lottery e-mail (where the target is told they have won a large prize but must pay an administration fee or provide their bank account details before they receive it). An example of the fake lottery scam is demonstrated below. Note how the scammers try to instil trust by stating that they want to ensure that it is the recipient of the e-mail (the 'real' winner) who wins the prize:

UK LOTTERY ORGANIZATION

TICKET FREE/ONLINE E-MAIL ADDRESS WINNINGS DEPARTMENT.

If you are the correct owner of this email address, then be glad this day as the result of the UK lotto online e-mail winning draws and sweepstakes held in DUBAI-UNITED ARAB EMIRATE on the 29th of September 2006 has just been released and we are glad to announce to you that your e-mail address has won you the lottery in the first category and you are entitled to claim the sum of US$4.6M.

Your email addresses was entered for the online draw on this Ticket Number:APP236566301307 and won on this Lucky Number: MX014926583.

You are to contact Mr. Timone Ong on the below email address for quick delivery of your won cheque of US$4.6M. All winners [sic] cheque are certified cashiers and are cashable in any country of any part of the world. To enable the Courier Company ascertain you as the rightful receiver of the cheque, include the below listed information in your contact mail.

Your country, complete official names, contact telephone, mobile and fax numbers, amount won, sex, age, occupation and job title, address where your wish to receive your winnings cheque, ticket and lucky number and lastly the date/venue of draw.

Top Speed Express UAE Company Ltd.
Office Address: 68 Naif Road, Dubai UAE.
Email-Address: . . .
Contact Agent: Mr Timone Ong.
Telephone: +971-50-565-2432.

N.B:

Even when you send all the above mentioned cliams [sic] information to the Top Speed Express, it wont be enough to get them 100% convinced that you are the rightful winner of the us$4.6m cheque without an original copy of your winnings certificate. This is because of the recent recording increase on fraudulent claims. On this note, to receive the original copy of your UK Lotto winnings certificate contact Mr Jerry Fidelix with your complete official names, amount won, ticket and lucky number, date/venue of draw on this below email address: . . .

Yours Truly,
Mr Jerry Fidelix.
Co-ordinator.
UK LOTTERY ORGANIZATION

Griffiths (2004) points out a few more online gambling scams, including the fake gambling site scam, the betting software scam, the gambling 'bonus' scam and the 'twofer' scam. The fake gambling site is simply a website that has copied parts or entire gambling websites. Given that individuals believe they are real websites they happily hand over their money to these sites and obviously do not win any money from them. The betting software scam is software that sells for one or two thousand pounds. The sellers claim that it can predict the outcome of horse races or lotteries. However, as Griffiths point out, it is impossible to predict the results of such random events. The gambling 'bonus' scam sends out e-mails to banned gamblers 'offering them a cash bonus if they deposit money into their existing account' (Griffiths 2004: 4–5). After they have deposited their money they are e-mailed to say they cannot receive the bonus as they have been banned from the site. These gamblers, according to Griffiths, still tend to play with their deposit at any rate, which of course is what the senders of the e-mail had counted on. The 'twofer' or 'two-for-one' scam is a fake online gambling site which tricks people into handing over their money. The site then closes and months later sends e-mails out to the previously scanned individuals (who do not realise the e-mail comes from the same site they had previously been conned by) and cons the same individuals into again depositing money into a fake online gambling site.

Phishing

Phishing is the attempt to get people to enter their username and password into a fake website, so that the information provided can then be later used fraudulently to access the person's real account. It usually begins with a mass e-mail (see Figure 6.1), which often requests that users validate their information by logging on to the organisation's website – except that the link provided does not lead to the official website but instead directs the user to a mock-up of the official site. The costs of phishing are difficult to ascertain. Some reports put the cost to UK consumers at £23.2 million in 2005 (Finextra 2006), and 1.2 million people lost almost $1billion in the USA (Kerstein 2005), while Leyden (2004) estimates the US cost at $500 million. What is certain is that this type of fraud is on the increase. The Anti-Phishing Working Group (APWG) reported that 14,191 unique phishing sites appeared on the Internet in July 2006, targeting 154 different brands. Around the same proportion of these sites contained either some form of the target brand name in the URL (46 per cent) as the number that

Dear Halifax bank customer,

We have implemented security measures consistent with our internal information security practices to help us keep your information secure. These measures include technical and procedural steps to protect your data from misuse, access or disclosure, loss, alteration or destruction.

One of these security measures is HOF (Halifax Online Form) to help us to keep your personal and banking data up to date.

You should complete HOF on a regular basis.

Please complete HOF using the link below:

Halifax Online Form

Halifax Automated Mail Service. Please do not respond to this mail.

Figure 6.1 Example of a phishing site

had no hostname, just an IP address (42 per cent). A phishing site was live for an average of 4.8 days – it is a hit-and-run form of deception.

Why does phishing work?

As a form of deception, phishing needs to convey to the unsuspecting user that the website they visit is credible and authentic. Dhamija *et al.* (2006) showed 22 participants a selection of websites, some legitimate, others phishing sites (some created by the authors, others 'genuine fakes'). They found that a good phishing site fooled 90 per cent of their sample. Almost a quarter of their sample used only cues from the website to determine its veracity (e.g. logos and layout) – they did not even look at the address bar to check the URL. This group scored the worst at identifying fake websites. A further 36 per cent of the sample used both the content of the website along with the URL address, but they did not look for signifiers of a secure site (e.g. https or a padlock icon). Dhamija *et al.* (2006) report one participant whose strategy was to enter their username and password into every site to see if it led to their account. When questioned about this, they said, 'What's the harm? Passwords are not dangerous to give out, like financial information is.' The website that fooled most of the participants (90 per cent) was a spoofed Bank of the West site with the URL www.bankofthevvest.com. This site convinced so many people for a number of reasons: only one person noticed the double v in the URL (as opposed to a 'w'). A large proportion of the sample (17) mentioned the design of the site, in particular an animation of a bear, which they felt would be 'too difficult' to spoof. The phishing site also linked to the genuine site's VeriSign security information. Dhamija *et al.* outline three main reasons for people accepting fake websites as real. The first is users' lack of knowledge, for instance, in the role of address bars, http versus https and secure sites, and so on. The second is through visual deception by phishers. They will copy the content and layout of a legitimate website, create URLs that look real (like bankofthevvest) or hide URLs behind images of genuine links. Finally, phishers take advantage of people's bounded attention; that is, users do not look for visual signifiers of legitimate sites and do not notice their absence. This is confirmed by research suggesting that security toolbars to warn people of potential phishing attacks are ineffective because people either ignore them or explain them away if the content of the site looks legitimate (Wu *et al.* 2006). In Chapter 9 we look in more detail at what factors create a credible, trustworthy website.

Spam

Spam is a nuisance form of e-mail that users receive on a fairly regular basis. Spam is essentially electronic junk mail usually sent out in bulk mailings to a large list of e-mail users. The scam e-mails mentioned earlier in this chapter are examples of spam. Other forms of spam are generally advertising products that often do not work – from penis enlargements to pharmaceuticals. It is perceived as a nuisance type of e-mail because it tends to waste people's time (trying to identify that it is junk e-mail and deleting it) and it uses up bandwidth. Businesses lose money because of spam as they waste hours of productivity due to spam taking up valuable bandwidth and slowing down systems. Moreover, they need to purchase filtering software to identify and cut down on the flow of these forms of e-mail. So, not surprisingly, this type of e-mail was named spam after the Monty Python song 'Spam spam spam spam'. Akin to the song, spam is a seemingly endless repetition of worthless text.

There are various types of spam and we tend to receive some more than others. SurfControl's Anti-Spam database reports that as of August 2006: 23 per cent of spam is products and services; 18 per cent is health and medicine; 17 per cent is finance and home business; 16 per cent is phishing and fraud; 14 per cent is adult entertainment; 12 per cent is not categorised. In most countries it is illegal to send spam. However, it still tends to clog up e-mail boxes on a regular basis. The reason why it exists is because it is successful. Powell (2003) reports estimates of 0.1 to 1 per cent of people who have purchased products from spam. He explains that although this might appear insignificant it provides a great deal of money given the number of people who are annually sent out mail.

Although spamming is a criminal activity it is not so easy to stamp out or catch the criminals. This is because of the way spammers send their e-mails.

Spammers sometimes send out viruses that infect computers, which in turn will connect to the Internet and download lists of e-mail addresses and send out spam in this way. Some people configure their servers incorrectly (as an 'open relay') and spammers send their e-mails to these open relay servers, which are then redelivered. The spam appears to come from the open relay servers. Spammers also purchase mail server services from ISPs using stolen credit card details which makes it difficult to trace them.

Although it is not easy to trace spammers, some have been caught out and even been sent to prison for their criminal activities. As reported on the BBC News (2005) website, 30-year-old Jeremy Jaynes was the first person in the USA to be given a prison sentence for selling sham products and services advertised via e-mail. He was making up to £398,000 per month for his criminal activity and at the time was said to be the world's eighth most prolific spammer. The BBC report stated that Jaynes was sending ten million spam e-mails per day. More recently, Kawamoto (2006) reports that two spammers in the USA, Jared Cosgrave and Mohammed Haque, could face a three-year prison sentence and a fine of up to $250,000. These two spammers were said to be sending spam through other people's e-mail accounts. They were accused of sending e-mails titled 'I'm finally back home' and 'I just got back in town'. These e-mails were said to contain messages that marketed herbal supplements.

Message-based deception

Message-based deception occurs when the identity of the communicant is known, and the deception occurs within the content of the communication. In everyday FtF or mediated interaction, this is the most common type. For instance, making up an excuse for being late (e.g. blaming terrible traffic when really you were in the bar), lying about your location (e.g. in the office versus at the golf course) or disguising your true feelings (e.g. saying that an awful outfit looks nice on someone) are all forms of message deception. Of course, this kind of deception is not necessarily a bad thing. According to DePaulo *et al.* (2003), in many cases deception can act to improve social cohesion and protect privacy (see also Chapter 11 where we discuss online privacy).

There have been a number of theories developed to predict in which type of media individuals are more likely to lie. For example, social distance theory argues that because lying makes individuals feel uncomfortable, they will choose leaner or less rich media in order to maintain social distance between themselves and the person they are lying to. That is, they will avoid media that contain cues which people believe will give away deceit (e.g. voice, body and language). Moreover, in less rich media the deceiver has more control over the interaction – any unexpected questions can be thought about, rather than being responded to immediately. If the social distance theory was supported by empirical research, we would find that people lie most in e-mail, followed by Instant Messenger, followed by phone and then FtF. Media richness theory, in contrast, suggests that because lying is highly equivocal individuals elect to lie more in rich media, which include multiple cue systems, immediate feedback, natural language and message personalisation. Hence, this theory predicts that individuals lie in FtF situations more, followed by phone, Instant Messenger and e-mail.

In respect to the four types of media just mentioned, Hancock *et al.* (2004) found that neither social distance theory nor media richness theory were supported. In their study they examined the lies of 28 students using a diary study running for seven days (where the participants record all instances of lies). The participants engaged in around six interactions a day, and lied on average 1.6 times a day (26 per cent of all social interactions included a lie). The most lies occurred during FtF interaction (n = 202, 1.03 per day), followed by telephone (n = 66, 0.35 per day), Instant Messenger (n =27, 0.18 per day) and e-mail (n = 9, 0.06 per day). The largest proportion of lies within a medium was via the telephone; the smallest proportion was in e-mail. Interestingly, the more experience people had with e-mail, the more lies they were likely to tell using that medium (a relationship that was not found for IM). Participants were also more likely to plan their lies by e-mail compared to FtF, but these lies were not rated as any more important (most were of the 'white lie' variety).

To explain their findings Hancock *et al.* (2004) offered a new theory, which they named 'feature based theory'. This theory adds three more dimensions that need to be considered when we examine deception – whether the medium is synchronous, recordless and distributed (i.e. not co-present). Feature based theory proposes that the more synchronous and distributed but the less recordable a medium is, the more frequently lying should occur. People lie more in synchronous interactions, because the majority of lying is spontaneous and hence synchronous communication should present more opportunities to lie. In recorded communication a person is aware that their conversation is potentially kept or stored (e.g. in a saved e-mail) and can be referred to in future conversations. Hence, people are less likely to lie if they are aware that there is proof of their lie which can be referred to later. In media where participants are not dis-tributed deception should be constrained to some degree as some lies can be immediately obvious (e.g. it is easier to lie in an e-mail saying one is writing a report when really one is playing a computer game).

Research since Hancock *et al.*'s (2004) study has found that the feature based theory does not necessarily hold when considering the target of the lie and the type of lie being told. Whitty and Carville (2008) asked 150 participants to rate on a Likert scale how likely they were to tell different types of lies across different media. They found that individuals were overall more likely to tell self-serving lies to people they did not know well. An example of a self-serving lie they used was:

You are having a FtF conversation with someone that you are 'close to' when they invite you to an event. You can think of something else you would rather spend your time doing so you tell them that you can't make it to the event, even though you can.

Whitty and Carville (2008) argue that it is more risky and difficult to get away with telling a self-serving lie to individuals who are close to us – given that people close to us have more information about our day-to-day lives. For self-serving lies told to people close to the participants or to those they did not know well, individuals stated they were more likely to tell a lie in an e-mail, followed by phone and lastly FtF. This result supports the social distance theory. Whitty and Carville explain that self-serving lies are more likely to make the liar feel uncomfortable and apprehensive, so e-mail is the ideal place to tell such a lie.

When considering other-oriented lies, participants were more likely to believe that they would tell these lies to individuals they felt close to. An example of an other-serving lie they used was:

You receive an email from a person you don't know well. Within the email they ask you if you think they look attractive. You don't think that they are attractive but you don't want to hurt their feelings so you email them back and tell them that they are attractive.

Other-oriented lies are typically told to protect the feelings of the target of the lie. Given this, a person might feel more compelled to lie to someone close to them to protect their feelings rather than saying the truth, which could possibly cause them upset or distress (Whitty and Carville 2008).

Participants in Whitty and Carville's study believed they would be just as likely to tell an other-oriented lie to someone close to them in any type of medium. Perhaps this is because the purpose of this type of lie is to maintain the integrity of the target and a person ought to be motivated to do this for someone they care about in any type of medium. Such lies are not told to hurt people but are intended to make others feel better about themselves. The more someone cares for another, surely the more motivated they are to utter such 'white lies'.

In contrast, when it came to telling an other-oriented lie to individuals they did not know well, the participants claimed they would be less likely to do it in an e-mail and most likely to tell this type of lie FtF. Again, this did not support the feature based theory, but instead was more likely to support the social distance theory. As Whitty and Carville (2008) state:

It is argued that people are more likely to talk aggressively in CMC (computer mediated communication) than face-to-face because online there is a lack of social presence and less contextual cues. This is perhaps why this current study found that individuals were more likely to say a hurtful truth than an other-oriented lie to individuals not well-known to them in email. The social distance, in this particular case, motivates the person to tell unpleasant truths.

How much lying takes place on the Internet?

The amount of lie telling found by Hancock *et al.*'s (2004) study is similar to that reported in earlier studies which consider offline communications (e.g. DePaulo and Kashy 1998). It also fits with other evidence of relatively minor interpersonal deception online. Caspi and Gorsky (2006) surveyed 257 users of 14 different newsgroups. Despite the majority holding the view that online deception was widespread, only around a third admitted to engaging in online deception themselves. Cornwell and Lundgren (2001) surveyed 80 chat room users, half about their 'realspace' relationships (i.e. offline relationships) and half about their cyberspace relationships. They found that 'realspace' relationships were considered to be more serious, and reported greater feelings of commitment to relationship than the cyber-relationship participants. Both groups, however, reported similar levels of satisfaction and potential for 'emotional growth' with regard to romantic relationships. Cornwell and Lundgren went on to ask whether the participants had misrepresented themselves to their partners in a number of areas: their interests (e.g. hobbies, musical tastes); their age; their background; their appearance; and 'misrepresentation of yourself in any other way' (p. 203). Participants responded using either yes or no to each question, and their score was summed into a misrepresentation measure. The results of the misrepresentation questions are shown in Table 6.2.

So the level of misrepresentation was remarkably low in both cyberspace and realspace relationships. The only significant differences in misrepresentation were for age and physical characteristics, which may represent degrees of freedom as much as anything else (it is difficult to misrepresent your appearance to someone sitting opposite you). The overall level of misrepresentation did not differ across conditions. Perhaps this is not surprising when considering relationships – if the intention is to meet someone

Table 6.2 Misrepresentation in cyberspace and realspace relationships (from Cornwell and Lundgren 2001: 207)

Misrepresentation	Cyberspace relationship	Realspace relationship
Interests	0.15	0.20
Age	0.23	0.05
Background	0.18	0.10
Physical characteristics	0.28	0.13
Other	0.15	0.05
Total score	0.99	0.53

in the future offline then large-scale deception would be discovered (Chapter 7 looks at online dating deception in more detail).

Detecting and preventing deception online

A number of technical solutions are currently in place to protect people from phishing, but no browser plug-in is going to stop someone meeting a purported Nigerian banker in a London hotel to hand over cash. In October 2006 Microsoft released its latest update to Internet Explorer (version 7) that incorporates a 'phishing filter' to warn users of suspicious sites. Whether this is going to work is open to question: as noted earlier, people tend to ignore warnings or discount them. Moreover, often the cues provided by browsers (e.g. a changed colour for the address bar when in a secure site) are too subtle for most users.

There is also evidence that deception is subtly given away in interpersonal communication. Savicki *et al.* (1996) analysed 2692 messages posted on 27 discussion groups for language content and gender. They found that groups involving higher proportions of men tended to use more fact-oriented language, while groups with higher proportions of females tended to show more self-disclosure and attempts at tension prevention and reduction. Herring (1993) reports that men tend to use more self-promotion, sarcasm, insults and strong assertions, and to post issue or information-related messages. Meanwhile, women are more likely to hedge, suggest ideas, express doubt and post personal topics and questions. Thomson and Murachver (2001, study one) asked 35 participants (19 females and 16 males) to send at least six messages to a 'net pal' of the same gender. The messages were then coded on linguistic style and content. The results indicated that females tended to post more references to emotion, more personal information about themselves, more models or hedges (e.g. I *sort of* agree with you) and more intensive adverbs (e.g. the game was *really* good). In a follow-up study, Thomson and Murachver (2001, study two) showed 78 participants a selection of messages from study one, and asked them to rate the gender of the author using a six-point scale (1 = definitely written by a female, 6 = definitely written by a male). Of the 16 messages shown, the gender of the author was correctly identified by a majority of participants for 14 (the percentage of correct answers ranged from 62 per cent to 95 per cent). It would seem then that the differences in language used by males and females do make identification of gender possible during CMC. Thomson and Murachver (2001, study three) also developed their own messages based on the criteria identified in study one. They found that gender predictions followed the use of language as anticipated. The 'female' message (which included an apology, an intensive adverb and emotion) was judged as more likely to be written by a female, while the 'male' message (which included an insult and longer sentences) was judged as more likely to be written by a male.

People might also use different communication styles when engaging in deception online. According to research by Zhou *et al.* (2004), liars use more words and these words are more informal and expressive, compared to people telling the truth. They also made more typographical errors. This finding was replicated by Hancock *et al.* (2005), who also found increased word count during deception in instant messaging. Interestingly, the people being lied to asked more questions than those being told the truth, perhaps suggesting that they knew, even subconsciously, they were being lied to.

Cyberslacking

Cyberslacking or cyberloafing 'is the overuse of the Internet in the workplace for purposes other than work' (Whitty and Carr 2006b: 237). This can often be hidden from one's employer (or at least the worker might believe it is hidden). This has been highlighted by some as a problem since it can potentially reduce productivity and therefore financial gain for an employer (Davis 2001; Davis *et al.* 2002). Greengard (2002) found that 56 per cent of employees were using the Internet for personal reasons. Similarly, Griffiths (2003) found that 59 per cent of Internet use at work was non-work related.

Unlike many other online deviant and deceptive behaviours, researchers are not all in agreement as to whether cyberslacking is in fact a problematic behaviour. For example, Whitty (2004b) found that, in the main, Australian workers believed that the Internet and e-mail should be used for non-work related purposes in the workplace. However, this was dependent on the types of online activities in which employees engaged. For instance, 61 per cent of her sample stated that employers ought not surf for or download offensive material such as pornography, discriminating, criminal or violent material. Similarly, Blanchard and Henle (2008) found that a group of American university students classified two types of forms cyberslacking: minor forms (e.g. sending and receiving personal e-mail at work as well as surfing mainstream news and financial websites and shopping online) and serious forms (e.g. visiting adult-oriented websites, maintaining one's own website, interacting with others online via chatrooms, blogs, and personal ads, gambling online and downloading music).

Various suggestions have been made for how to deal with cyberslacking. Using monitoring software to spy on one's employees has been one suggestion (Davis 2001). Making more transparent workplace policies has been another suggestion (Goldring *et al.* 2001). A further way to deal with the problem, according to Davis *et al.* (2002), is to use preventative measures such as identifying the workers who have problematic Internet use. These theorists understood problematic use to be determined by four indicators: impulsivity, loneliness/depression, distraction and social comfort. As an alternative view, others have argued that not all Internet personal usage should be dissuaded and that, ironically, it could in fact increase productivity (Whitty and Carr 2006b). For example, surfing the web could be a more contemporary form of having a break, which in earlier days might have been more likely spent around the water cooler. Moreover, conducting some personal online activities such as online banking can take up far less time than having to physically get to a bank. Further research is needed, however, to determine exactly what personal online activities ought to be permitted in the workplace.

Motivation for deception

On the Internet, not all deception is anti-normative or unhealthy. Indeed, in many cases it might be considered perfectly normal to engage in identity play (for instance, when taking part in a massive multiplayer game). Playing in cyberspace can be formative rather than necessarily detrimental (Whitty 2003a; Whitty and Carr 2006a, 2006b). Danet (1998), for instance, has argued that cyberspace can be liberating for women if gender is masked or neutralised. Whitty (2003a) has stated that it can be therapeutic to play at reconstructing presentations of self online. In particular, she believes that playing with a variety of possible identities, especially physical identity, can be therapeutic for some individuals – especially for shy and unattractive individuals. People might also be drawn to the Internet to tell particular kinds of lies. Hancock (2007) argues that highly motivated liars are less likely to be discovered online compared to FtF. Utz (2005) argues that it is important to take into account the reason for the deception. Deception, as noted, can also be a method for maintaining privacy or avoiding unwanted attention. The choice of a misleading or deliberately ambiguous pseudonym or other forms of identity concealment, while potentially deceiving, is also critical to preserve privacy (Utz 2005). Utz also reports that the perceived malicious intention of the deceiver influences the perceived severity of the deception.

Conclusions

As we have seen in this chapter there are many different ways we might be lied to in cyberspace. Some of this deception is highly illegal and can cause a great deal of grief for those who are taken in by the lie. The chapter has dealt with a range of lies – including scams and fraud, as well as lies people more commonly tell in their everyday lives. One of the important notions we have emphasised in this book is that to truly understand the Internet we need to look at its different parts. Some people are more likely to lie in different places online more than others. In the following chapter we look in more depth at deception in one space online – online dating sites.

7   Short, light and ugly

Misrepresentation of the self in online dating sites

In Chapter 6 we discussed how individuals or groups deceive others on the Internet. We also touched upon the sorts of lies people might tell their online partners. This chapter considers lies told to potential romantic partners on the Internet by examining how online daters present themselves on online dating sites.

Online dating

Online dating sites began appearing in the 1980s and are currently the most popular way to meet romantic partners in cyberspace. Yahoo.com claims almost 380 million visitors per month to their online dating site (Pasha 2005) and FriendFinder.com say they have over 2.6 million active members (Dating Sites Reviews.com, n.d.). These numbers are continuing to grow. As described in Chapter 3, online dating sites are quite similar to newspaper personals in that individuals are required to provide information about themselves and the type of partner they are looking for. There are, however, some important differences. People can and are usually required to add more detail than newspaper ads. Individuals can be matched through tools developed by the online dating company and through their own searches (e.g. searching for certain characteristics and demographic details they are looking for in a partner). There is more visual and sometimes auditory information displayed on the profiles (e.g. photos, video and sound bites). Getting to know one another via online sites is also different in that people can indicate and test the attraction of another in a more subtle way (e.g. via a short note delivered through the site often given a flirtatious name, such as a kiss or a wink). From there individuals might elect to e-mail each other via the site, where they can then move to phone and FtF if they so choose.

There is a variety of types of online dating sites. Some require their clients to complete personality tests, as well as surveys on their interests and what aspects they are looking for in a partner. Next, matches are often given compatibility ratings. Sometimes individuals seek out matches on the sites themselves and are given a compatibility rating with their choice. At other times the site selects a compatible profile from their database for individuals to consider. More specialised online dating sites exist that gather like-minded individuals together. For example, there are sites designed specifically for Christians, Jews, vegans, goths or spiritual people. Such sites are similar to social groups one might join in the hope of finding another who shares the same values or interests. Moreover, Whitty (2007b) argues that these sites potentially cut out some of the work in the search for the perfect other. This is because individuals can at least believe that they share many similarities with others who use the site. Such sites could also lead to greater trust in others who use the site (which is a challenge for many online dating sites, as this chapter will highlight)

How honest are online daters?

As with other spaces online, researchers have been interested in how truthful individuals are to potential dates via online dating sites. They have also been exploring which aspects of themselves individuals elect to present on these sites and which of these aspects are more likely to lead to budding relationships. Unfortunately, even though online dating sites are spaces where individuals are typically not visually anonymous (since they usually display a picture of themselves) some individuals have been known to misrepresent themselves on these sites – even about their physical appearance. As Whitty (2007a, 2007c, 2008; Whitty and Carr 2006a) reports from her interview study, online daters recalled that when they met dates from an online dating site some had lied on the site about the following characteristics:

- looks (including describing themselves as better looking than they really are, outdated photos, a photo of a different person)
- weight/size
- personality
- age
- height
- their intentions (e.g. looking for people just for sex although claiming to be looking for people for a long-term relationship)
- SES (socio-economic status: education, occupation, income, being professional)
- relationship status (did not admit on profile that they are married).

Similarly, Hancock and colleagues (2007) have found that individuals admitted to lying about their weight and height in their online dating profiles. For two-thirds of their participants, weight was inaccurate by five pounds or more. Women were more likely to lie about their weight and men more about their height.

Some of the participants in Whitty's research reported more than little white lies being told to them. A number recalled some hellish dating

experiences where their dates turned out to be very different from the way
they described themselves on the site, including being presented with a
photograph of a different person. Examples include:

R   Oh yes. One lady I met once described herself as slim and she had
    to be a size 18 at least. I didn't even recognise her and she came
    over to me and she said 'are you Rob' and I said 'yes' and she said
    'I am such and such' and I just went white.

                                        (*Rob*, Whitty and Carr 2006a: 140)

S   Another gentlemen, his profile looked good, we spoke on several
    occasions, we met and what I saw in the profile was different to
    what I saw face-to-face.
I   So his photo was different?
S   Yes . . . he was ten years older than what his photo was and I am
    thinking in my head, hang on a minute, you look like this yet your
    photo shows me that you are a younger man, not that I am after a
    younger man but the photo, I could see the similarities in the face-
    to-face person, but I was totally disappointed. Why can't people
    just be honest?

                                    (*Sophia*, Whitty and Carr 2006a: 140)

C   It was just for a drink down in a club in the area.
I   And you say that it was unsuccessful, so why was it unsuccessful,
    how did that date go?
C   Because he was nothing like his photo, he was nothing like what he
    sounded in his emails or on the phone. He just name dropped the
    whole time, and I don't know whether he was nervous and he was
    just trying to impress me or what, but, I wasn't comfortable with
    him.
I   So his photo was really different, in what way was it different?
C   It was his brother.
I   Oh it was the brother. And so did he give an explanation as to why
    he was a different person.
C   No, he just said he put his brother's on because they looked
    similar.
I   And so he also didn't click well with you either you are saying?
C   Well he was short and fat and bald.
I   And his brother is not?
C   No

                                (*Christine*, Whitty and Carr 2006a: 141)

Others reported lies that were more subtle. Interestingly, the participants
were often equally unhappy with these dates. Whitty (2008) argues that the
reason for this is because daters would judge even those who slightly

misrepresented themselves as disingenuous people. If someone tells 'white lies' on Internet dating sites they are still typically judged as an untrustworthy person. Examples of some of the more subtle lies include:

> T   Some I found that told a whole lot of dribble, let's face it, the people who tell the truth you want to be the ones you want to be interested in. So, like there is so many, what I have found that I have met women there, they have put their age on there and when you actually meet them they have actually been 2 to 5 years older than what they have said on there.
>
> *(Tom*, Whitty 2007a: 66)

> B   I find that 6 foot 2 is a lot shorter these days than it used to be.
> I   So men lie a little bit about the height?
> B   Yes I think height tends to be one area that has been a little bit of a mislead.
>
> *(Bronwyn*, Whitty 2007a: 65)

The penalty for lying on an online dating profile, according to Whitty's participants, was to abruptly end the development of the relationship. Even if the lies were not major deviations from the truth, the online daters still felt that they could no longer trust the person.

Trust is important in establishing and maintaining relationships. It increases security in a relationship, reduces inhibitions and defensiveness and increases openness. Given that online daters are already putting themselves in a vulnerable position by self-disclosing more than they normally would when first meeting someone, trusting another's self-disclosure is obviously extremely important. Moreover, many of the more experienced online daters reported being deceived and as a consequence becoming more cautious when it comes to trusting a profile.

Indicators of trust

So how do online daters decide which profile to trust? The research to date suggests that they seek out 'indicators of trust'. Lawson and Leck (2006) have identified the presence of early and late trust indicators used by online daters. For example, they found that online daters looked for verification of age by looking at clothing style, hairstyle and projected lifestyle in individuals' photographs. In addition, when it came to e-mailing, online daters claimed to be able to look for age indictors in the style of writing. For example, they reasoned that younger people are more likely to use acronyms (e.g. BRB – 'be right back') and abbreviations in their online conversations.

Lawson and Leck (2006) argue that another indicator of trust is the timing or flow of self-disclosure and the progression of the online relationships to offline. Some online daters felt uncomfortable with individuals who self-disclosed much more quickly and wanted to move the relationship faster than would normally happen in FtF scenarios. They give an example from a 25-year-old salesman that they interviewed who stated:

> Internet people are more desperate; things move fast in weird ways. . . . It [meeting online] sets you off on a weird path. You get too intense too soon. There's like a speed to get to know each other. All you have is conversation that becomes exaggerated and magnified. It becomes drama . . . One woman I met online said, 'I think I am ready for a relationship now.' This scared me. I wanted to just maybe have at least one date in person and get to know her better before committing to a relationship.
>
> (Lawson and Leck 2006: 15)

Whitty's research mentioned above also revealed indicators of trust (Whitty 2007a, 2008; Whitty and Carr 2006a). For example, the online daters in her research typically avoided profiles that contained 'cheesy clichés'. This was because they deemed these profiles as less 'real' than other profiles. As the quotations below illustrate, participants were perturbed by cliché-type profiles and avoided them because they saw them as untrustworthy:

> T I tend to stay away from those people with sort of cliché stuff. I think it appears in a lot of profiles . . .
>
> I What would be some of the clichés that you would be turned off by?
>
> T With some, on some profiles it has a very sexual overtone, which puts me off totally. Sometimes it is like a passage of clichés, walks on the beach, romantic evenings, romantic getaways, a bottle of wine, and nice crackling fire. It just doesn't ring true, it just sounds like a, it doesn't seem very real.
>
> (*Teresa*, Whitty and Carr 2006a: 143)

> G And everyone says that they like walking on the beach, and anyone will tell you that it is so god damn boring [laugh]. And when they say that I think 'oh my God, not another one, it is almost a turn off'.
>
> I They are all on that beach walking [laughing].
>
> G Oh my God, if there are so many on that beach walking, why don't they run into each other.
>
> I So a bit cliché that one?
>
> G Terrible, it is almost a turn off now.
>
> (*Grace*, Whitty and Carr 2006a: 143)

Players are a type of online dater that is typically not trusted on Internet dating sites (Albright 2007; Whitty 2007a, 2008; Whitty and Carr 2006a). This is someone who sends out many e-mails on an online dating site hoping that at least one person will respond (often referred to as a 'numbers game'). This type of person typically does not read the profiles and typically is a man. Most women in Whitty's study were unimpressed with this sort of person as they felt they were not being singled out as someone the player honestly wanted to date, but that rather the player was desperately seeking out any date. Many of the women reported receiving e-mails from men that they believed were obviously 'form e-mails' as they did not point out the characteristics which they found attractive or appealing in their profiles. Moreover, some women stated that they went to great lengths to point out they were not interested in certain types of men (e.g. smokers or drinkers) and yet men who said they smoked and drank heavily still contacted them, suggesting they had not read their profile. Some of the women from Whitty's research report:

S   I wonder if the guys do [read the profiles], I think the girls might but I don't think the guys necessarily do because it's too much hard work. . . . But it also means that you see someone's profile and you think, well 'I think that you have just randomly picked me out of a hat, but I don't think that you have really done a proper search.'

(*Susie*, Whitty and Carr 2006a: 139)

I   So you get the impression that they are not even reading your profile?
J   Not that they are not reading it, but just that they are just mass kissing [sending out mass e-mails through the site] everyone, it's like an orgy of kisses [orgy of mass e-mails] [laughs]. It's just stupid, whoever thought that up, I just think that it is really dumb.

(*Joan*, Whitty and Carr 2006a: 139)

The men in Whitty's study also owned up to playing 'the numbers game'. Unbeknownst to them about how women might interpret their approach, they believed that this strategy would lead to success and did not consider that women might judge them as insincere and untrustworthy. To give an example:

I   Do you contact many people and just hope that one will respond?
A   Yes, it's a numbers game. Between you, me, and the gatepost mate, life is a numbers game and you win some and you lose some and unless you are in their pitching you ain't going to get nothing.

I OK

A You select those that obviously there is some interest and some similarity, commonality, and pass the rest by, but still it's a numbers game.

I Right

A You look at the picture and you read the words, and if it is better than 50 per cent you send them a kiss [e-mail through the site].

(*Alan*, Whitty and Carr 2006a: 138)

One final indicator worthwhile considering in more detail is the photograph displayed on the profile. As mentioned earlier in this chapter, Lawson and Leck (2006) have found that people look at the photograph in a profile to verify age and projected lifestyle. In Whitty's (2007a) study some of the men pointed out that they were suspicious of women with 'glamour' photographs (i.e. photographs taken by a professional photographer) because they believed that in 'real' life they would probably not live up to expectations. As expressed by the following men:

M You could go and get portrait photos taken and they spend three hours putting concrete on your face and fill all the gaps so photos aren't always a good guide.

(*Martin*, Whitty 2007a: 98)

G I'm just looking at one now that talks about body type and it says average and yeah that looks like it is but the photo that is there is a glamour photo and it's been taken professionally and yes she's all dolled up and she's got all make up on her and everything like that and that's fine. But I bet she's not going to look as good as that just to meet for coffee.

(*George*, Whitty 2007a: 99)

Meeting FtF

A screening out process

The indicators of trust that online daters look for on a profile are clearly not enough. Given the lack of trust in others online, daters typically want to meet up within a few weeks of initial contact (Whitty and Carr 2006a). They also want to meet up to establish chemistry and potentially to begin a relationship. However, the first date is less of the traditional romantic style first date and instead seems to be more of a screening out process. Even the place that they decide to meet appears set up more for an interview situation (e.g. coffee shop, bar or shopping centre) than an actual date, as aptly described by the following online daters:

I   Where do you arrange your meetings?

J   Generally a public place like cafés, we try and pick a significant spot that's easy to meet, like on the corner of something or outside a particular store. We just go there and head off for coffee. It's usually coffee, I don't think I've ever actually met anybody first other than coffee, it's always been coffee.

(*Jeff*, Whitty and Carr 2006a: 136)

L   I meet him at a shopping centre. I always meet them in a very open place during the day.

I   And why do you do that?

L   I wouldn't meet a stranger in a dark alley. I have this image of meeting strangers in dark alleys or whatever so I thought in a coffee shop or a restaurant if it is a nice place.

I   And this is for safety reasons?

L   Yes.

(*Lisa*, Whitty and Carr 2006a: 136)

Online daters appear to choose these locations for safety reasons (as they do not entirely trust their date) as well as for a quick getaway if their date does not meet up with their expectations. This is explained by online daters Shane and Belinda:

S   I suspect that in that first couple of weeks there wasn't too much trust involved and partly by that stage I had had enough experience of meeting, of having these Internet connections, and I was very suspicious of . . . I was very aware that I shouldn't subject anything into them so until we had actually met you know.

(Shane)

B   This is a person . . . didn't have a photo on his profile. I had e-mailed him and we spoke to each other only once but we got along quite well. We meet for coffee over a lunch break so it was nice and short and you had an excuse to go back to work if it wasn't a successful meeting.

(Belinda)

Lies or a different presentation of self?

Since the beginnings of the Internet, theorists have been interested in how individuals present themselves online. Researchers have claimed that individuals can be very experimental and playful with their presentations of self (Whitty 2003a). Those who hold this view believe in multiple selves, rather than the notion that there is one unitary self. It has been argued that reduced auditory and visual cues allow individuals to be more strategic and creative with presentations of self (Suler 2000; Whitty and Carr 2006a); moreover, that cyberspace is a unique space that allows individuals to learn more about their identity. Turkle (1995), for example, is well known for her view that MUDs and MOOs presented opportunities for people to experiment with multiple identities. Others have examined the ways individuals decide to present themselves on their own web pages (e.g. Miller and Arnold 2001). Miller and Arnold found that women academics struggle with establishing a credible presence on their personal web pages. In respect to adolescents, it has been found that young teens can be very experimental with their presentations of self, with girls presenting themselves as more beautiful and boys pretending to be more macho than they are in reality (Valkenburg *et al.* 2005).

So rather than arguing that individuals are deliberately presenting false versions of themselves online, it might be more likely the case that many online daters believe their profiles are versions of the truth – one way of presenting who they are to others. As Whitty (2007a, 2007c, 2008) has argued, online daters often believe they are strategically presenting a more attractive version of themselves rather than an 'inauthentic' self. Many of the people she interviewed explained that they hoped that in so doing they would attract a greater number of potential dates. This strategy, however, seems to unravel once they reveal a more accurate depiction of the self. This is clearly explained by Danny:

D   This is the thing. I still had my pre-97 photos on the site and this is where it started to become a little difficult where, they would look at the pictures and they would think 'I want me a piece of that' and then they would get the recent photo and they would go 'Yuck' and not very subtly either. For example, you would be in a lengthy conversation, hoping that personality wins, then they would get the photo. You might be up to the telephone conversation stage or beyond, you might actually meet to have coffee and once they meet you and have coffee with you, or they see a recent photo of you, it's 'Oh I found somebody else' or you just lose contact.

I   That is a bit hard isn't it.

D   Especially coming from where I had been. Pre-97 I sort of basically had my pick.

(*Danny*, Whitty 2007a: 100)

Theorists have been concerned with which presentations of self online are more likely to lead to budding relationships (e.g. Bargh *et al.* 2002; McKenna *et al.* 2002; Whitty 2007a). Bargh *et al.* (2002) and McKenna *et al.* (2002) have argued that cyberspace allows one to reveal one's 'true' self, the true self being the traits or characteristics that individuals possess and would like to but are not typically able to express. This they compare with the 'actual' self, which they define as traits or characteristics that individuals possess and express to others in social settings. These theorists have found that individuals who are able to express their true selves rather than their actual self in newsgroups are more likely to develop romantic relationships online and more likely to progress these relationships to the offline world.

The theory proposed by Bargh *et al.* (2002) and McKenna *et al.* (2002), however, does not appear to predict the success of online daters (Whitty 2007a, 2008). Online daters seem to be hyper-concerned with honesty and the search for genuine people on the site. They appear to be far less concerned than individuals in newsgroups with a gradual revealing of a 'true' self. Instead, as explained above, if an online dater did not live up to their profile the relationship ceased to progress. Given this approach Whitty (2007a, 2008) has proposed her Balance between an Attractive and a Real Self (BAR) theory, which recognises that individuals are strategic when they construct their profiles. This theory suggests that the best strategy to employ is to present a balance between an 'attractive self' and a 'real self'; that is, to make one's profile stand out and appear unique and interesting but also to be a profile that individuals can live up to in the first FtF encounter.

Romance scam

This chapter has demonstrated that some online daters do misrepresent themselves on online dating sites. Often their intentions are simply to find a date rather than for any malicious purposes. There are, however, a growing number of individuals who are joining sites to con people into a romantic connection with the intention to scam money from them.

Chapter 6 outlined the now well-known Nigerian scam. The romance scam is another version of this scam. One might even go so far as to say that it is a more sinister version of the scam. Like the Nigerian scam, these scams seem to originate from Africa (especially Nigeria) as well as Russia, eastern Europe, Thailand and the Philippines. The person might also claim to be American or British and working abroad in one of these countries.

In contrast to the Nigerian scam which relies on individuals' greed to lure victims, the romance scams plays on desperate individuals' need for love. For this scam to work the scammer must first attempt to create a strong emotional tie with their victim. To lure their victims they create a profile on an online dating site or on sites such as Myspace with a photograph of a highly attractive person, typically using stolen photographs of models. They construct profiles on every sort of dating site, including mainstream ones, as well as religious, gay and professional sites. Although they will target anyone, typically they will go for middle-aged men and women in professional jobs (as they have money to part with) and those looking for long-term relationships. When they contact the person through the site they use persuasive and flattering words and poetic language. They often use pet names to establish intimacy and claim that fate or a higher power has pre-ordained the romance. Once they have caught their victims' interest, they invite them to chat using IM and typically will always use a free e-mail service such as Yahoo or Hotmail as this makes it much more difficult to trace the person. They quickly declare love and express a strong desire to be physically present with their victims. They will send the target copious amounts of romantic e-mails and even gifts (bought with stolen credit cards). This is usually carried out by groups of individuals who together work on the right things to say to ensure their target will fall deeply in love with them. Phone calls might also be made, and when the scammers are only men they bring in female confederates to make the phone call to the male victims.

The grooming period might continue for four months, but has been known to continue for over a year or longer. This period ends when the scammer successfully proposes to their target. At this point the victim is primed with thoughts of long-term happiness with their new love. The scammers continue this priming by painting a picture of the possible future. The scam kicks in when the scammer reveals that he is living abroad (e.g. Nigeria) and that for a whole host of reasons does not have sufficient funds to make the trip (e.g. problems with the Nigerian banking system to cash their work cheques) to be with their beloved. At this stage, the victim is very prepared to help out and will often comply with the scammer's request to cash in cheques and post back the money. Of course the cheques are forged or stolen and the scammer attempts to get the victim to cash in as many cheques as they can before the bank figures this out and places a freeze on the victim's account. The scammer will also tell the victim to keep a portion of the money for themselves. They do this to establish trust as well as to incriminate the victim in the hope that this will reduce the chances that they will report the scammer to the authorities, since if they accept a portion of the funds they will then appear to be an accomplice.

There are a number of other versions of this scam. Many of these variations scam the victim of their own money. For example, some of the scammers ask their victims to lend them money to enable them to purchase a ticket and cover departure taxes with the promise that this money will be repaid once the couple finally meet. Some might request cash advances from the victim's credit card and offer to pay the balance – where the victim then offers up their credit card security information. Other scammers purchase expensive goods off eBay and ask the victim to pay for them by sending money to diverse locations throughout the world.

Individuals these days are more likely to be conned by a romance scam than the classic Nigerian scam. This is in part because smaller amounts of money are involved, the motivation is for love and the romance scam is not as well known as the classic Nigerian scam. Support groups have been set up online for those who have been conned and there are sites with photographs used by the scammers to help alert online daters to them.

Conclusions

Although this chapter demonstrates the various problems that individuals encounter with deception on online dating sites, it should be highlighted that many have managed to develop successful relationships with individuals they have met on these sites. The success, as this chapter suggests, might be down to how they decide to present themselves. Using the correct strategy is critical. Being honest is of utmost importance, but so too is presenting an interesting and enticing profile. Success might also be down to how savvy online daters are in deciding which profiles are genuine and which are less honest or outright scams.

8   Cheating with a mouse
Internet infidelity

> For many months my wife's use of her laptop has been increasing. She
> spends more than a 150 hours a month on-line. I know she has been chat
> cheating and it led to at least 2 physical contacts out of the country. She was
> foolish enough to save some of her memorable chat sessions on disks and I
> found them. I have been devastated. We have 2 children 11 & 14 and our
> entire lives have suffered from this. I confronted her and we have just begun
> counseling. She still goes online whenever she can so I think I need moni-
> toring software.
>
> (Anonymous, Cheating wife stories – cheating husband stories)

The previous two chapters considered deception on the Internet. This
chapter continues to look at the dark side of cyberspace by considering how
people might use this space to cheat on their offline partners. The Internet
is replete with stories about people who have engaged in cyber-affairs.
Internet infidelity has accounted for a growing trend in divorce cases (Baker
2005). Support groups for aggrieved spouses are sprouting up online and
monitoring software has been developed to check up on one's suspected
cyber-cheating spouse.

There is a range of places, as well as a range of ways, to cyber-cheat on a
partner. Some people might engage in anonymous cybersex in chat rooms,
while others might develop online romantic relationships with people they
have met online and perhaps never intend to meet offline. Sites have been
set up online for married people to engage in cybersex with other married
people. For example, the site Meet2cheat has written an introduction to
their service:

> We will be happy to advise you concerning the seriousness and reli-
> ability of our company. The idea of bringing private individuals, who
> have no interest in financial gain, together for sexual adventures
> through the Internet started already in 1997. The comprehensive
> concept and the idea of facilitating affairs and erotic adventures of all
> kinds nationally and internationally required a preparation period of

over a year. In April 1998 we were finally able to offer our service as one of the first of its kind in the Internet.

(Anonymous, Meet2cheat)

Others might use the Internet to locate a person for a discrete offline affair. For example, Philanderers.com is an online service which is an introductory agency for people seeking an extramarital offline relationship. They write on their site (note the ironic twist with the site's claim to value honesty):

> Why you are here is our main concern. Helping you sort out your thoughts, provide some direction for your extramarital affair, and a safe, secure outlet for your extramarital desires is our mission.
>
> We are not a sex or personals site that provides empty promises. Our clientele are well educated and informed before they become members. We are not 'the biggest', 'the best' or the 'most popular' – we don't want to be. We are honest, forthright and caring. Three things that we value in our extramarital web-relations.
>
> Come in and explore. Learn why you may want to pursue an extramarital affair and what you can do about it. Find out the reasons why this may be just the right place for you. Find out how you can fulfil your extramarital desires.
>
> (Anonymous, Philanderers.com)

Given the apparent number of ways people can cheat on their spouse online, what do psychologists have to say about online infidelity? Do they claim this to be a healthy innocent encounter or do they believe extramarital online sex and relationships to be a real form of infidelity?

Is Internet infidelity a real form of betrayal?

It was clinicians who first began to speculate that cyber-relationships could be *'real'* affairs (e.g. Cooper 2002; Maheu and Subotnik 2001; Young 1998; Young *et al.* 2000). In the main they concurred that engaging in online sexual activities and developing online relationships were 'real' acts of betrayal if one is already in a relationship. In attempting to define Internet infidelity, Shaw (1997) has stated that 'Internet infidelity is, of course, behaviorally different from other kinds of infidelity; however, the contributing factors and results are similar when we consider how it affects the way partners relate' (p. 29). More specifically, Young *et al.* (2000) defined a cyber-affair as 'a romantic and/or sexual relationship that is initiated via online contact and maintained predominantly through electronic conversations that occur through e-mail and in virtual communities such as chat rooms, interactive games, or newsgroups' (p. 60). In contrast, Maheu and Subotnik (2001) provide a generic definition:

Infidelity happens when two people have a commitment and that commitment is broken – regardless of where, how or with whom it happens. Infidelity is the breaking of a promise with a real person, whether the sexual stimulation is derived from the virtual or the real world.

(p. 101)

Non-clinical samples have been consulted for their opinions on whether certain Internet activities might be considered as relationship transgressions (e.g. Mileham 2007; Parker and Wampler 2003; Whitty 2003b, 2005; Whitty and Carr 2005a). These authors conclude that some online sexual (e.g. cyber-flirting and cybersex) and emotional activities (e.g. sharing intimate secrets and falling in love) are thought to be acts of online betrayal.

Whitty (2003b) surveyed individuals about their attitudes towards online and offline infidelity. Overall, 1117 respondents rated whether they believed certain activities were acts of betrayal. These participants were recruited both online and offline. The study considered acts such as sexual intercourse, cybersex, hot chatting, emotional disclosure and pornography. The research found that individuals do believe that some interactions that occur online are acts of infidelity. Some of these behaviours, such as cybersex, posed a greater threat than other behaviours such as downloading pornography. The study also found that there are separate components of infidelity which researchers need to consider, including sexual infidelity, emotional infidelity and pornography.

In a follow-up study, Whitty (2005) employed a qualitative method to investigate people's representations of Internet infidelity. Drawing from a study conducted by Kitzinger and Powell (1995) on offline infidelity, Whitty devised a story completion method where participants were asked to write a story in response to a cue relating to Internet infidelity. This study found that emotional infidelity was stressed as much as sexual infidelity. In this same study, Whitty (2005) examined the kind of impact participants believed that cyber-cheating could have on the offline relationship. Sixty-five per cent of the stories mentioned that the aggrieved had been hurt or upset by this virtual encounter. In many cases participants wrote that the online infidelity led to a break-up of the relationship. Whitty concluded from this study that some online interactions could potentially have serious repercussions on the offline relationship.

Parker and Wampler (2003) asked 242 undergraduate students to rate scenarios on degrees of whether they thought they were an affair. The scenarios included: meeting someone in a hotel room to have sex; interacting in adult chat rooms; having cybersex; having telephone sex; becoming a member of an adult website; engaging in cybersex various times; visiting adult chat rooms but not interacting; and visiting various adult websites. These researchers found that all of the sexual activities they included in their survey, except for visiting adult chat rooms but not interacting and visiting adult websites, were viewed as acts of infidelity.

In another study Mileham (2007) interviewed 76 men and 10 women which she recruited from Yahoo's *Married And Flirting* and MSN's *Married But Flirting* chat rooms. Married people inhabit these sites and engage in cyber-flirting and cybersex and sometimes organise to meet offline. Although Mileham does not clearly state in her paper exactly what she asked these participants, she claims that some of these participants acknowledged that online activities could be perceived as unfaithful. In her study, most of the types of infidelities that appear to be identified as unfaithful were sexual activities online, such as cybersex.

How can virtual sex be 'real' infidelity?

The mounting evidence does suggest that most individuals consider cyber-cheating as a 'real' form of infidelity. Nevertheless, it is fair to ask: Why is cybersex regarded as a real form of cheating if it is only *virtual* sex? To answer this question it might be helpful to consult previous research on offline infidelity.

Sexual intercourse is not the only sexual activity that individuals consider as infidelity. For instance, Roscoe *et al.* (1988) found that undergraduates believed that engaging in other sexual interactions with someone else, such as kissing, flirting and petting, ought to be considered unfaithful. Yarab *et al.* (1998) revealed an array of unfaithful sexual behaviours in addition to sexual intercourse, including passionately kissing, sexual fantasies, sexual attraction and flirting. Interestingly, Yarab and Allgeier (1998) found that when considering sexual fantasies, the greater the threat of the sexual fantasy to the current relationship, the more likely the fantasy was rated as unfaithful. For instance, fantasising about a partner's best friend was considered by most to be more of a threat, and therefore more unfaithful than fantasising about a movie star.

Returning to the question posed above, the empirical research outlined here suggests that it is the sexual desire for another which is the act of betrayal. Hence, displays of that sexual desire as well as fantasising about the object of one's desire can be upsetting for one's partner. Of course, not all sexual activities are deemed as equally upsetting. Whitty's (2003b) research, for instance, found that sexual intercourse was rated higher as an act of infidelity than cybersex. Hence, penetrative sex might be seen as a fait accompli and therefore more upsetting than other sexual activities.

Not all about sex: emotional infidelity

The research on offline infidelity also demonstrates another type of infidelity – emotional infidelity. Emotional infidelity is understood to be falling in love with another individual other than one's partner, or sharing intimate and/or secret details about oneself with someone one is attracted to other than one's partner. Yarab *et al.* (1998) have argued that 'mental exclusivity' might be considered to be as important as 'sexual exclusivity'. Their empirical evidence supports this notion. In addition to sexual activities, their participants viewed the following as acts of infidelity: non-sexual fantasies about falling in love; romantic attraction; behaviour in dyads, such as studying, having lunch with and going to a movie with someone other than one's partner.

Research on Internet infidelity has also found evidence to support the notion that individuals believe that falling in love with someone online or sharing intimate details with another online are acts of infidelity. This is illustrated by one of the female participants in Whitty's (2005) study where participants were required to write a story to a cue about Internet infidelity:

> 'It is cheating'. She said rather calmly.
>
> 'No I'm not cheating. It's not like I'm bonking her anyway. You're the one I'm with and like I said I have NO intentions of meeting her.' He hopped into bed.
>
> 'It's 'emotional' cheating.' She said getting annoyed.
>
> 'How so?' He asked, amusement showing in his eyes.
>
> 'Cheating isn't necessarily physical. That's one side of it . . .' He pulled the sheets over him and rolled over.
>
> 'Well . . . I know you have not met her yet that's why, but I'm still a little annoyed, Mark.' She sat on the edge of the bed.
>
> 'Don't be mad. You're the one I love. So how is it emotional cheating?' He sat up.
>
> 'You're keeping stuff from me. Relationships are about trust! How can I trust you if you keep stuff from me about the "Internet' girl"?'
>
> (pp. 62–63)

Gender differences: which is worse – sex or love?

The general consensus has been that men and women hold different viewpoints on offline monogamous relationships. For instance, Sheppard *et al.* (1995) have argued that men tend to view commitment and monogamy as less attractive options than women do. It also seems that men and women enter into extramarital relationships for different reasons: women more because they are seeking a friendship or emotional relationship, while men tend to be more interested in sexual relationships (Glass and Wright 1985). Satisfaction within a marriage is also often marked by these gender differences, with men more likely to report sexual problems, and women more likely to indicate problems with affection as the cause of discord within the marriage (DeBurgher 1972).

Men are more likely than women to at least own up to having some type of extra-dyadic sexual experience (Hansen 1987; Townsend and Levy 1990). Yarab *et al.* (1998) found that men admitted more than women did to fantasising about having sexual intercourse and giving and receiving oral sex with someone else other than their partner. Moreover, men in their study were more likely to state that they had 'hit on' someone else.

Overall, it seems that men and women do not differ in the amount or how regularly they experience jealousy or upset in regards to infidelity (Buss 2000). Nonetheless, some researchers have found that men and women differ in the 'weighting given to the cues that trigger jealousy' (Buss 2000: 46). As Buss (2000) explains: 'Men are predicted to give more weight to cues of sexual infidelity, whereas women are predicted to give more weight to cues of long-term diversion of investment, such as, emotional involvement with another person' (p. 46). This he explains through an evolutionary lens. According to this theory, through natural selection the human species has inherited certain traits and emotional reactions. Researchers such as Buss contend that ancestral man faced a grave threat from cuckoldry – that is, uncertainty about the paternity of their partner's children. Consequently, men are likely to respond with more intense jealousy to sexual infidelity than women. Ancestral woman, on the other hand, faced the risk that an unfaithful male partner might divert his resources to another woman and her children. Therefore women have developed an innate jealousy towards emotional infidelity (the assumption being that the man will expend resources on the 'other woman' they are in love with).

Research on offline infidelity has indeed found that, when forced to choose whether sexual or emotional infidelity is most upsetting, women more than men rate extra-dyadic emotional behaviour as more upsetting (Shackelford and Buss 1996). Some have found this result even when participants are not forced to decide. For example, Roscoe *et al.* (1988) asked participants to list what behaviours they believed were relationship transgressions. In this study men were more likely to state that a sexual encounter with a different partner was an exemplar of infidelity. In contrast, women were more likely to state that spending time with another and keeping secrets from a partner were acts of infidelity. It is, however, worthy of note that both men and women report extra-dyadic sexual behaviour to be more unacceptable and a greater betrayal than extra-dyadic emotional behaviour (Shackelford and Buss 1996).

Not all theorists agree with evolutionary theorists' accounts for infidelity. For example, DeSteno *et al.* (2002) have argued that the methodology Buss and his colleagues use to test out their claims is not sound. One reason for this is because the results are not always found when individuals are presented with scenarios separately with rating scales (as opposed to the forced choice of deciding between which is worse – sexual or emotional infidelity). The gender differences either do not occur or on occasion there is a shift in the opposite direction (with women reporting more jealousy towards sexual infidelity).

Alternative theories have been developed to explain the jealousy and upset experienced from betrayal. For instance, some theorists have contended that existing gender differences need not reflect innate modules. Instead they might be better explained by a social-cognitive approach as well as developmental theory (e.g. DeSteno and Salovey 1996; Harris 2004; Harris and Christenfeld 1996). Such theorists believe it is crucial to understand what men and women read into their partners' infidelity. This has been named the 'double-shot hypothesis' (DeSteno and Salovey 1996) or the 'two-for-one hypothesis' (Harris and Christenfeld 1996), which essentially argue that a man feels doubly upset thinking about their female partner having sex with another man as he holds the belief that to do so she is most likely in love with the 'other' man. Hence, sexual infidelity implies emotional infidelity. Women, in contrast, think that men can have sex without being in love and so do not believe that sexual infidelity implies emotional infidelity. Instead, women get the double hit if they think their male partner is in love with another woman. This is because they believe that emotional infidelity implies sexual infidelity. Men, however, do not assume that their female partner is having sex with another man that they are in love with. Therefore, they do not experience any additional upset from this thought.

To test out their claims, Harris and Christenfeld (1996) asked their participants to think of a serious romantic relationship they had been involved in and to imagine that this partner has been engaging in sexual intercourse with someone else. On a five-point Likert scale participants had to rate the likelihood that their partner was in love with the person they had sex with. In addition, they were again asked to think of a serious romantic relationship they had been involved in and to imagine that their partner was in love with someone else. On a five-point Likert scale participants had to rate the likelihood that their partner was having sex with the person they were in love with. As predicted they found that men were more likely to say that their partner was in love with the person they were having sexual intercourse with and women were more likely to say that their partner was having sex with the person they had fallen in love with.

In an attempt to replicate Harris and Christenfeld's (1996) study, Whitty and Quigley (in press) only found part support for their 'two-for-one hypothesis' (see Table 8.1). They found that men assume that if their partner is having sex with another man then she is very likely to be in love with the other man, and that women do not assume that if their partner is having sexual relations with another woman then he is in love with her. However, they did not find support for the second part of the hypothesis, that is, women are more likely to believe than men that if their partner is in love with someone else they are likely to be having sex with them. Whitty and Quigley (in press) argue that their results probably differ because sexual attitudes and practices have changed since Harris and Christenfeld's study. Moreover, they contend that if the results do reflect a change in social shifts then in turn they provide more support for a social-cognitive model, rather than a socio-evolutionary explanation.

Gender differences on the Internet

So what of gender differences when it comes to attitudes towards online infidelities? Consistent with previous research on offline infidelity, Whitty (2005) found that women, more than men, mentioned emotional betrayal in their stories of cyber-infidelities. In line with previous research on offline betrayal (e.g. Amato and Previti 2003; Paul and Galloway 1994), she also found that women were more likely than men to write that they would end the relationship if they found out their partner was having an Internet affair. Moreover, the women in Whitty's (2005) study were more likely than the men to talk about the time and distancing from the relationship the infidelity caused.

Interestingly, as with some research on offline infidelity, when presented with scenarios separately with rating scales the gender differences have been found to occur in the opposite direction. Parker and Wampler's (2003) study, which considered sexual online activities, found that women viewed these activities more seriously than men did. Whitty's (2003b) study found that women overall were more likely to believe that sexual acts were an act of betrayal than men did.

Whitty and Quigley (in press) also considered whether the 'double-shot hypothesis' or the 'two-for-one hypothesis' applied to attitudes towards cyber-infidelities (see Table 8.1). Their research did not find any gender differences or any support for these hypotheses. Moreover, they found that participants were much less likely to believe that cybersex implied love or that online love implied cybersex than they were to believe that sexual intercourse implied love or that love implied sexual intercourse. They argue that this could be for a number of reasons. First, given that previous research has found that most people have not engaged in online sexual activities, then making connections between love and cybersex is not so easy to do. Second, given that cybersex is qualitatively different to sexual intercourse then, although individuals might still perceive it as a relationship transgression, they do not necessarily link it with love in the same way they would with offline relationship transgressions.

Age differences

Little is known about age differences in experienced romantic jealousy and distress caused by emotional and sexual infidelity. This is because in the main researchers have drawn from a college sample, which typically consists of young adults. Nonetheless, evolutionary theorists have predicted age differences in distress caused by emotional and sexual infidelity (Shackelford *et al.* 2004). They contend that older men would be distressed less than younger men by a partner's sexual infidelity. This is based on the assumption that their partner is a post-reproductive woman. In contrast, they predict that older women would be less distressed by emotional infidelity when compared with younger women. This is based on the assumption that older

Table 8.1 Means and standard deviations of participants' ratings of how much sexual infidelity (on and offline) implies emotional infidelity and how much emotional infidelity (on and offline) implies sexual infidelity (adapted from Whitty and Quigley in press)

Gender	N	Sex implies love	Love implies sex	Cybersex implies love	Online love implies cybersex
Women	61	3.16	3.51	2.74	3.03
		(1.25)	(1.09)	(1.15)	(1.10)
Men	51	3.71	3.67	2.71	2.76
		(1.19)	(1.11)	(1.36)	(1.21)
Total	112	3.41	3.58	2.72	2.91
		(1.25)	(1.10)	(1.25)	(1.15)

women are less likely than younger women to have dependent children and hence less likely to require resources to support their offspring. Researchers such as Shackelford *et al.* (2004) are quick to point out that they are 'not proposing that the evolved jealousy mechanisms are "undone" with age but, instead, that these mechanisms may have age-sensitive design features' (p. 62). In testing out this theory Shackelford *et al.* (2004) compared a younger sample with a mean age of 20.2 years and an older sample of 67.1 years. Contrary to what they predicted, they found no significant differences between young men and older men for distress felt by sexual infidelity. However, in support of their thesis younger women were more distressed by a partner's emotional infidelity when compared to older women. In attempting to explain why the older men did not decrease in sexual infidelity, Shackelford *et al.* (2004) speculate that this might be because their partner was still at an age when they could reproduce. They also suggest that future research ought to consider the possibility of cohort effects.

Research on Internet infidelity has also considered age differences in attitudes towards infidelity. Whitty (2003b) found that 23–44-year-old men were more likely to rate online and offline sexual behaviour as acts of betrayal when compared with 45–70 year olds. In contrast, older women (45–70 year olds) were more likely to rate online and offline sexual infidelity as a form of betrayal than younger women (23–44 year olds). Whitty also found the difference within age groups varied depending on whether individuals were in a relationship or not. For instance, younger people (17–22 year olds) in a relationship rated online and offline sexual infidelity higher as a form of betrayal than younger people (17–22 year olds) not in a relationship. The same pattern was found for the 23–44-year-old group. However, the reverse was found for the oldest group (45–70 years). Whitty concludes her study by suggesting that cohort effects ought to be investigated. What these studies suggest is that when it comes to romantic jealousy and upset caused by infidelity the research needs to move beyond focusing on gender differences.

Breaking the rules

An alternative approach to understanding infidelity comes from theorists who contend that individuals develop scripts or knowledge structures about the world, which Fitness (2001) describes: 'As children grow to become adults, they learn from their caregivers and culture what relationships are all about – that is, they acquire theories, or knowledge structures, about relationships and how they work' (p. 74). She argues that over time partners acquire many relationship scripts in respect to their varied routines, and how to resolve conflict as well as other emotional interactions, including jealousy:

> The process and outcomes of interpersonal betrayal may also be regarded as a form of interpersonal script in that people hold socially shared beliefs about the kinds of behaviors that constitute acts of betrayal and expectations about the ongoing thoughts, feelings and behaviors of both parties to the betrayal.
>
> (Fitness 2001: 78)

Fitness argues that when partners play by the rules and meet each other's expectations then their relationship runs smoothly. Infidelity is an example of where couples do not play by the rules and expectations are not met.

Although individuals might have scripts available to them as to what are acceptable FtF interactions with the opposite sex while still maintaining a romantic relationship, given the nature and newness of the Internet the rules are yet to be clearly established as to what are acceptable online encounters (Whitty 2005; Whitty and Carr 2006a). Arguably couples' relationship scripts when it comes to online interactions are not so clearly defined. Although, as demonstrated in this chapter, individuals hold similar attitudes towards online and offline infidelities, the current literature does suggest that online the rules are less clear. For example, in Whitty's (2005) work, referred to earlier in this chapter, individuals were presented with a hypothetical scenario of a partner potentially cheating online that not all participants were convinced was 'real' betrayal. Participants were given one of two versions of a story-completion task based on a task devised about traditional offline infidelity by Kitzinger and Powell (1995):

> *Version A*: Mark and Jennifer have been going out for over a year. Then Mark realises that Jennifer has developed a relationship with someone else over the Internet.
> *Version B*: Jennifer and Mark have been going out for over a year. Then Jennifer realises that Mark has developed a relationship with someone else over the Internet.
>
> (Whitty 2005: 59)

Kitzinger and Powell (1995) found that 90 per cent of their sample interpreted their cue story, which was developed in respect to offline infidelity, to be an act of sexual involvement. However, this was not the case in Whitty's (2005) study where all of the participants understood this to be a dilemma about infidelity. However, some were divided as to whether the betrayer believed they were committing an act of infidelity, while others wrote that the partner was not certain that they had been betrayed. Moreover, unlike Kitzinger and Powell's study, when participants interpreted the cue story as a story about sexual involvement, this was not necessarily about a sexual relationship, but in many cases was exclusively an emotional involvement.

Although the majority of participants (86 per cent) in Whitty's (2005) study wrote that the aggrieved felt that they had been betrayed, and 51 per cent wrote that the betrayer believed that they had been unfaithful, a number of participants were uncertain that this was a scenario about infidelity. Explanations given as to why the scenario should not be considered as infidelity included:

- the interaction was 'just a friendship'
- the interaction was merely flirtation or fun
- the relationship was with an object (computer) in virtual space, rather than with a real human being
- the interaction was with two people who had never met and did not ever intend to meet
- it could not be infidelity as there was no physical sex taking place.

Of course most of the statements above could also be used to justify offline encounters that one's partner might interpret as betrayal. Nonetheless, the participants in Whitty's (2005) study were more likely than Kitzinger and Powell's (1995) participants to find rationales for why the scenario was not 'real' infidelity. This might be explained by individuals' lack of scripts of acceptable online behaviour.

Counselling implications

Theorists have speculated as to what the best forms of treatment might be for those who cheat on their spouse. Unfortunately, some of these treat the spouse who cheats as having a sexual compulsion or addiction, which is not always the case (Whitty and Carr 2006a). Delmonico *et al.* (2002) argue that there ought to be two phases to treatment. The first step should be treated as a crisis intervention, where clients should reduce their Internet access and avoid problematic sites or web pages. In the second phase clients need to have their rituals interrupted. To do so, Delmonico *et al.* (2002) suggest that clients need additional psychiatric evaluations: their social isolation, stress and grief need to be addressed; and family support should be increased.

Not all infidelity treatment rationales focus on just stopping the behaviour from occurring. Instead, others suggest that therapy should also consider problems between the couple. Maheu and Subotnik (2001), for example, suggest that interventions should include communication training. Gonyea (2004) proposed that therapy should include increasing intimacy between the couple. Hertlein and Piercy (2006) have suggested that during the assessment phase the couple's idiosyncratic rules for the relationship should be addressed. In the following treatment phase they argue that the therapist should examine the behaviour around the Internet infidelity, focusing especially on anxiety, differentiation and triangulation.

In a review of the literature on Internet infidelity, Hertlein and Piercy (2006) argue that more empirical research is needed to devise improved treatment rationales for this new problem. They suggest that this ought to be carried out even if researchers only have access to small samples. Hertlein and Piercy believe that therapists should all adhere to a specific framework. Second, they suggest that common factors used in marital and family therapy should be employed, such as assessing the couple's optimism and commitment to change.

Conclusions

Obviously psychologists need to carry out further research on cyber-cheating in order to find out exactly which acts cause the most upset, what motivates people to cyber-cheat, how online relationship transgressions affect the offline relationship, and the best treatment rationale for this problem. Gender differences also need to be further investigated. However, it is safe to conclude at this point that cyber-cheating is a 'real' form of betrayal. As Whitty (2005) has argued, despite the lack of the physical self in cyberspace, online sexual and romantic activities can have a real impact on one's offline relationship.

9 Building trust through communication

Bargh and McKenna (2004) describe using the Internet on many occasions as a 'leap of faith' (p. 586). Purchasing online compared to a bricks and mortar store requires a belief that the goods will arrive, that they will be as described on the website and that your credit card and personal information will not be traded or otherwise misused. If we contact a potential partner via an online dating site, there is no knowing if they are as they have described themselves in their profile or subsequent communication. When we work in virtual teams, or join virtual communities, we take it on faith that the people we talk to are who they say they are. When we seek advice online, we often do not know who are the authors of the advice we receive and what motivates them to help us.

In these kinds of scenarios, trust is critical in determining people's behaviour. The concept of trust has been studied in many different disciplines, and there are a large number of potential definitions (Corritore *et al.* 2001; Green 2007). However, it is generally agreed that trust is critical when there is a degree of uncertainty (Mayer *et al.* 1995). This uncertainty also needs to contain an element of risk (Deutsch 1962). Without any risk or vulnerability, there is no need for trust (Mayer *et al.* 1995).

Mayer *et al.* (1995: 712) define trust as 'the willingness of a party to be vulnerable to the actions of another party based on the expectation that the other will perform a particular action important to the trustor, irrespective of the ability to monitor or control that other party'. Put more simply, it is the 'willingness to be vulnerable, based on positive expectations about the actions of others' (Bos *et al.* 2002: 1). In an interpersonal context, it can be defined as holding 'confident expectations of positive outcomes from an intimate partner' (Holmes and Rempel 1989: 188) or 'an expectancy held by individuals or groups that the word, promise, verbal, or written statement of another can be relied on' (Rotter 1967: 651).

Trust takes many forms. It can be a personality trait or disposition, with some people more trusting than others (Mayer *et al.* 1995). It is also an attitude or belief about the intentions of a specific other (McKnight *et al.* 1998). It can be generalised (you trust a person or group across all domains) or specific to an interaction (you trust a person only in one domain). So, you might not trust real estate agents in general, but you do trust the one you hire. It also has cognitive, affective and behavioural components (Lewis and Weigert 1985), and might arise from heuristic or systematic processing of information about the trustee (Sillence *et al.* 2006). There is general agreement that trust is best conceptualised as multidimensional (Bhattacherjee 2002; Gefen 2002; Mayer *et al.* 1995). That is, trust comprises a number of unique aspects that, while interrelated, are also discernable.

Bhattacherjee (2002) identifies three main dimensions of trust: ability, integrity and benevolence. *Ability* refers to the knowledge, skills and competence of the person trusted to conduct the expected actions. In an e-commerce setting, this might be the expectation that an online store has the ability to take an order and process it, and will do so without accidentally revealing personal information. According to Bhattacherjee, this dimension of trust is domain specific: that is, trust in one area (e.g. to provide the book we ordered) does not transfer to other domains (e.g. we would not necessarily trust Amazon to provide us with health advice). The second dimension, *integrity*, refers to the belief that the person or institution will act in an honest, reliable and credible manner (Jarvenpaa *et al.* 1998). That is, they will adhere to the usual rules or expectations perceived as fair to both parties, and will not violate the trust placed in them (i.e. you have confidence in the person or organisation you are trusting). In an interpersonal context, integrity would reflect your confidence that the person you are trusting will not violate that trust, and it has a strong element of predictability (i.e. you have confidence in how the other person will behave in the future). In an e-commerce context, integrity would refer to a belief that the organisation you are dealing with is honest, reliable and will keep its promises (Gefen 2002). Finally, *benevolence* refers to 'the extent to which a trustee is believed to intend doing good to the trustor' (Bhattacherjee 2002: 219). In a commercial setting, this might be reflected in beliefs that a company has its customers' best interests at heart (although this does not rule out making a legitimate profit). Benevolent organisations do not make excessive profits, or exploit their customers. In an interpersonal setting, benevolence would refer to the belief that the person giving you advice is doing so to help you, not themselves (or a third party).

Why trust is important

As we have noted above, on the Internet we often take a leap of faith that the people or organisations we deal with can be trusted. Moreover, lack of trust is a problem for online organisations: 'if the web site does not lead the consumer to believe that the merchant is trustworthy, no purchase decision will result' (Ang and Lee 2000: 3). A survey by Harris found that the three biggest consumer concerns in the area of online personal information security were: companies trading personal data without permission; the consequences of insecure transactions; and theft of personal data (Harris

Interactive 2004). Earlier, Hoffman *et al.* (1999) reported that almost 95 per cent of Internet users declined to provide personal information when requested to by a website, and over 40 per cent provided false demographic information when asked. But this is not a direct link between privacy concerns and behaviour – instead, there is considerable evidence that the link between privacy and behaviour is mediated by people's trust in the organisation (e.g. Chellappa and Sin 2005; Malhotra *et al.* 2004; Metzger 2004; Nickel and Schaumburg 2004).

Interpersonally, trust is also important. Developmental psychologist Erikson argued that a key part of a healthy personality was 'basic trust' (Erikson 1963: 7). Trust is also essential for cooperation (Deutsch 1962) and for effective teamwork, whether FtF or mediated (Bos *et al.* 2002). Trust is also critical in understanding when we choose to share with others and when we choose secrecy. Altman (1977) describes a *self boundary* (the boundary around the person) that is modified by self-disclosure and a *dyadic boundary* that ensures the discloser's safety from leakage of information to uninvited third parties. Trust is critical in establishing the impermeability of the dyadic boundary. According to Derlega and Chaikin (1977), people function within a dyadic boundary perceived by a person as a safe zone within which to disclose to an invited other and across which disclosure does not pass, either at the time of disclosure or subsequently. They argue that when the personal boundary is closed, private information is withheld. When it is opened the individual discloses to others so long as the dyadic boundary is closed. The self boundary may be open or closed depending on such interpersonal factors as the level of trust in a disclosure target (Altman 1973).

For people seeking advice online, a trustworthy source is also critical. A recent Pew Internet and American Life Project (2006) found that 58 per cent of Americans caregivers rated the Internet as the most important information source in caring for a loved one. Furthermore, in choosing the sites to use trust is a critical issue (Williams *et al.* 2003).

Trust and interpersonal interaction

Handy (1995) stated that 'trust needs touch' (p. 46). This reflects the widely held belief that trust between people is poorly established in lean, mediated environments (e.g. Bos *et al.* 2002). As we have seen earlier in this book, the Internet provides opportunities for people to engage in various forms of deception, ranging from creative self-presentation to the creation of fake identities. In such circumstances, it is perhaps not surprising that many commentators have seen the Internet as a difficult place to build trust.

Trust is also critical to the development of romantic relationships (Green 2007). According to Rempel *et al.* (1985), trust in romantic relationships has three components: predictability, dependability and faith. In the early stages of a relationship, the focus is on *prediction* – understanding the other person and their goals and motives. As the relationship develops, this becomes more about the person and their qualities and characteristics, rather than their actions (i.e. their *dependability*). The final component, *faith*, is the belief that future interactions with people we have yet to know can be trusted.

There are a number of techniques that people engage in to build trust in interpersonal computer mediated communication. These techniques vary depending on which space online individuals are meeting one another (Whitty and Carr 2006a; Whitty 2007c, 2008). For example, in Chapter 7 we examined important indicators of trust that online daters look for prior to any communication with the person who supposedly matches up to a particular profile. Moreover, online daters typically move to a FtF meeting fairly quickly (often a few weeks to a couple of months) after initial online contact on the site (Whitty 2008; Whitty 2007a). One of the reasons for this is to verify that the person matches up to their profile (Whitty 2007a).

So how is trust established in spaces such as newsgroups and chat rooms where individuals are unknown to one another? People are often visually anonymous when communicating in these spaces and begin with knowing far less about an individual than they would when compared to the first interaction with someone on an online dating site. Hence, it is perhaps more difficult to trust the identity revealed by people one might meet in these spaces. How does one know that their cyber-mate will not turn out to be a 40-year-old man after they have described themselves as an attractive, slim, blonde 18-year-old?

Researchers have found that on the Internet individuals go about reducing uncertainty by asking more direct probing questions (Tidwell and Walther 2002). If this is responded to with heightened self-disclosure and reciprocated (Joinson 2001), then a virtuous cycle of hyperpersonal inter-action might occur (Walther 1996). The use of profiles, and particularly photographs, is also designed to increase the level of trust at an interpersonal level while simultaneously reducing uncertainty (Tanis and Postmes 2007; Whitty 2007a, in press a; Whitty and Carr 2006a).

People also use linguistic cues to convey trustworthiness. Galegher *et al.* (1998) examined the messages of three Usenet support groups and three hobby groups collected for a three-week period to look for clues as to how their members established legitimacy and credibility. The group members created legitimacy in a number of ways. They posted messages appropriate to the group and used snappy headers to make themselves 'heard'. Galegher *et al.* note that often posters refer to their own membership of the electronic group, or how long they have lurked for, before asking a question/replying to one. Even frequent posters included references to their membership of the group 80 per cent of the time when asking questions. Posters also often signal their membership of the specific problem group (e.g. depression) by introducing information on their diagnosis, prescription or symptoms. In the support groups Galegher *et al.* studied, 80 questions received no reply. Virtually all of these lacked any legitimising information of the type outlined above, and were generally simple requests for information rather like complex database queries. In the hobby groups, evidence of such legitimacy seeking was much less apparent.

For those posting information, seeking to convey authority or at least limiting the potential reach of any disagreement seemed to be more important than establishing legitimacy. Galegher *et al.* (1998) found that people answering questions used a number of techniques either to limit the potential comeback on questionable advice, or to establish authority. Many posters included caveats in their replies (e.g. 'here's my two cents worth' or 'YMMV – your mileage may vary'). These caveats were mainly used when someone's answer was based on their own personal experience. For answers that attempted to establish a scientific or factual authority, the posters would tend to citations (e.g. to studies or professional organisations) or refer to their own background. If a reply lacked these markers of authority and was not based on personal experience, it was likely that its authority would be challenged in a follow-up message.

Within pseudonymous environments, reputation systems also provide an important marker for a person's trustworthiness (Resnick *et al.* 2000). The most well known reputation system is that used by eBay (which we discuss in more detail later in this chapter). In the eBay system, users leave positive, neutral or negative feedback, plus a short comment, for each transaction. Resnick and Zeckhauser (2001) studied the eBay reputation system and reported that although a very small proportion of the feedback they analysed (less than 300 instances from over 36,000 cases in total) was negative, the feedback did seem to predict the sellers' future success, including the chances that their goods would be bought.

With the rise of social computing and Web 2.0 sites, reputation systems have spread, such that it is now common to find community systems with rankings for members based on (among others) longevity, number of postings and (for the highest ranks) a form of peer review. Many of the blog commenting systems also now incorporate systems for reader rating of comments.

A further method to increase trust in interpersonal interaction is media switching. As we have noted earlier, Internet relationships tend to follow a similar pattern of initial contact in a public arena, then to a private domain (e.g. e-mail or AOL messenger), then to the telephone and then to FtF meetings (McKenna *et al.* 2002; Parks and Floyd 1996; Whitty and Gavin 2001). This movement is not only a signifier of trust (I trust you enough to give you my phone number), but also a way in which identities can be established, and the *faith* shown earlier is rewarded with *predictability* and, perhaps, *dependability*.

Media richness theory might explain the choices to move from chat to e-mail to telephone to FtF. This theory proposes that individuals often want to overcome equivocality and uncertainty (Daft and Lengel 1986; Trevino *et al.* 1987). Rich media are media which have availability of instant feedback, capacity to transmit multiple cues, use of natural language and a personal focus on the media. According to this theory, FtF communication is the richest type of medium as it provides immediate feedback and utilises more channels. The telephone would be less rich, followed by other types of media such as IM and e-mail. When it comes to meeting people from the Internet, individuals would obviously want to overcome equivocality and uncertainty before a decision to meet is agreed by both parties. However, while there is the desire to eliminate equivocality, there is also the need to protect one's identity until certain that they trust the other enough to provide more information and reveal more of their identity. This is perhaps why we see the progression of online relationships moving from less rich to more rich media. Moreover, this might explain why online daters like to meet their date fairly early on after initial contact on the site.

Trust in virtual teams

As noted earlier in this chapter, there is a common conception that 'trust needs touch'. To examine this, Bos *et al.* (2002) compared trust ratings and co-operation between team members across four different conditions: FtF, audio conferencing, video conferencing and text chat. The three-person teams were playing a trust game where co-operation maximised the potential gains for all members, while a competitive strategy reduced the likelihood of a higher gain. Bos *et al.* predicted that trust would be lowest, and performance impeded, in the lean media condition. Their results confirmed their predictions: the text chat groups scored the experience lowest in trust, and gained the lowest amount of points in the game (signifying a competitive strategy). However, the Bos *et al.* study may not be strong evidence for trust needing touch. First, the experimenters banned social conversation from the experiment. This immediately placed the 'richer' media conditions at an advantage since visual and aural cues normally compensated for in CMC social communication could not be used in this sterile environment. When social chat is allowed in such environments, trust levels improve (Zheng *et al.* 2001).

Second, and related, such games are artificial in the extreme and have little relationship to how people actually use media (Riegelsberger *et al.* 2003; see also Chapter 2). Third, the time given to the experiment was not sufficient for the text-based condition to 'catch up' with the media with faster communication exchange (Walther 1992). Finally, the use of self-reports for trust is unreliable, since people tend to rate richer media as higher in trust, despite evidence that communication is more effective without identity cues for experienced users (Tanis and Postmes 2007).

Trust and Internet websites

As also noted earlier in this chapter, trust is critical in e-commerce. Without trust, there will be no purchase. One very popular e-commerce site is eBay.

However, given the risks involved in buying and selling online, how has it managed to become so popular? Online auctions such as eBay are similar to their offline counterparts in that potential buyers need to bid for sellers' wares. Almost anything can be sold on eBay, with only a few types of items barred from sale on the site (e.g. anything illegal, religious relics or serial killer art). Individuals who choose to sell their goods on eBay list and describe the items and typically display a photograph of the item for sale. Sellers will set a minimum bid and decide on the length of the auction. They also need to disclose where they are willing to ship the items, shipping costs, acceptable forms of payment and whether or not to set a reserve price. Once the auction is over, both seller and buyer can leave positive, negative or neutral ratings and write a short sentence feedback. Everyone who logs on to the eBay site can view these ratings and feedback.

So what is so risky about eBay? There are risks for the seller, the buyer and for the site itself. Take for example the following stories. On 16 October 2006, the news.com.au website ran a story about unsafe infant products such as used cots, high chairs and car restraints being sold on eBay (News.com.au 2006). The article claimed that few of the items they spotted are safe by today's Australian product standards. Moreover, it claimed that it is virtually impossible to prosecute or enforce penalties on sellers that were not selling their wares in Australia.

On 25 September 2006, the BBC News site ran a story titled 'Boy, three, buys car on the Internet'. The article reports that a three-year-old boy bought a £9,000 Barbie-pink Nissan Figaro on eBay. The boy's mother revealed that she had left her eBay password on her computer and her son used it clicking the 'buy it now' button. Fortunately for the parents, the seller saw the funny side of the situation and did not expect them to purchase the car.

On 16 September 2006, Perkins (2006) reported on the commercial appeal website that a man from Memphis together with other US online auctioneers on the eBay website were being sued by the film industry for movie piracy. Perkins writes that 'previous lawsuits indicate online auctioneers who sell counterfeit DVDs on eBay have made an estimated $100,000 [US dollars] over 19 months'.

On 29 August 2006, the BBC News site ran a story titled 'eBay car buyer robbed at gunpoint'. The article reports that a 23-year-old man living in Sussex was the successful bidder for a Mercedes on eBay. When he went to east London with the £5,500 he agreed to pay for the car, he was approached by four men, one of whom produced a gun. The victim was forced to hand over his money without seeing the supposed car he purchased.

As illustrated in the stories above, one of the risks for the seller is the legitimacy of the bid and whether the buyer will actually pay up. As Boyd (2002) reports, one of the problems for sellers on eBay is that underage bidders occasionally drive up auction prices with no intention of paying. Another risk for the seller is the possibility that the buyer might leave undeserved negative feedback.

There are also a number of risks for the buyer. As demonstrated in some of the news stories, there is the possibility that they are unknowingly purchasing stolen and/or unsafe goods. Buyers are also only presented (and not always) with a picture of the product they are considering purchasing. They need to trust that the goods are not damaged and live up to the photo and/or description given on the website. Buyers also need to trust that the seller will not leave undeserved negative feedback. However, the biggest risk for buyers is a loss of privacy and security. For instance, one's eBay account might be hacked into and used to purchase items for other individuals. One's personal information such as credit card details could be stolen. Of course, these are similar problems to other online sites, such as social networking sites, where individuals also tend to provide too much information about themselves to the public or strangers that can easily lead to 'Internet fraud'.

The risk for eBay and similar auction sites (or other sites such as social networking) is that they could gain a bad reputation – a reputation as an unsafe, risky place to sell and buy goods or provide other services to the public. Negative press and enough negative feedback from others could bring it into disrepute. So how does eBay, in particular, ensure that it maintains a good reputation? Given that it is a risky place for both buyers and sellers on the surface, this would seem a difficult task. Boyd (2002) points out that eBay claims its success is down to its emphasis on community. He writes that 'the rhetorical construction of "community" on the site provides a foundation for the trust between users'. In fact eBay (n.d.) has set out five basic community values:

> eBay is a community where we encourage open and honest communication between all of our members. We believe in the following five basic values.
>
> We believe people are basically good.
> We believe everyone has something to contribute.
> We believe that an honest, open environment can bring out the best in people.
> We recognise and respect everyone as a unique individual.
> We encourage you to treat others the way that you want to be treated.
>
> eBay is committed to these values. And we believe that our community members should also honour these values – whether buying, selling, or chatting. We hope these community values will help you better understand the eBay community.

Boyd (2002) has pointed out that some critics have argued that 'although eBay calls itself a community, such a designation might be self-serving but inaccurate'. Rather, as he suggests, there seems to be some tension between community and commerce and that to resolve this tension one needs to accept eBay as a community of commerce.

It cannot be denied that eBay has to date been a success. However, this does not mean that all people feel completely safe or that it has ceased to be a risky activity. The above stories are testament to some of the problems that buyers and sellers might encounter. Those who do not feel completely safe in this environment use strategies to minimise their risk. In an article published in August 2006 on the online version of *Sydney Morning Herald* it was revealed that the independent Communications Law Centre found that most Australians spend less than $500 on any item on Internet auction sites to avoid losing too much in scams. Importantly, the report also revealed that 48 per cent of people who completed their survey had experienced problems when buying one or more items at an online auction website. Forty six per cent stated they had paid for an item which they never received and 41 per cent received an item that was different. Of concern was the finding that four out of ten wronged buyers have either never successfully resolved the problem, or received satisfactory results only a few times. So in conclusion, while eBay and many other similar types of online auction have been successful, it is still nonetheless a risky activity and many individuals encounter problems with using the site.

Trust is also critical for other kinds of sites. For instance, in social networking sites you trust that the personal data you enter into the system will not be released or misused by the host of the service. In seeking advice online, we would want a trustworthy source not compromised by lack of knowledge or bias. For many organisations, the mechanism to establish trust has been to pursue a 'clicks and mortar' approach of combining an offline presence (and brand recognition) with online presence. However, for Internet online services this has not been either possible, desirable or the route chosen. So how do these services establish trust?

Initially, it was argued that the Internet would provide a level playing field for small and large retailers alike (Watson *et al.* 1998). However, given the need to establish trust, it would seem that organisations with an existing reputation are at an advantage. Jarvenpaa *et al.* (2000) found that for bookstores and flight bookings the perceived size and reputation of the company determined consumers' likelihood of purchasing from it. The reason for this is that increased size and reputation led to higher trust, which in turn influenced the perception of risk and the willingness to buy.

How people assess trust in sites

Sillence *et al.* (2006) argue for a three-stage model for understanding how people assess the trustworthiness of a website. Stage one assumes that people are faced with a large number of potential websites (in their example to seek health advice), and thus engage in rapid, heuristic-based analysis on the design of the site rather than the content. At the second stage, people engage in a more systematic analysis of the content of the site, during which time they are influenced by the apparent integrity, benevolence and exper-

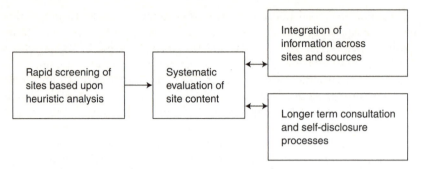

Figure 9.1 Staged model of trust (adapted from Sillence *et al.* 2006)

tise demonstrated (Bhattacherjee 2002). Stage three is a relationship development and integration stage; that is, a person's continued use of a site, personalisation and the integration of experience. This model is shown in Figure 9.1.

Design and trust

A critical part of the first stage of assessing trustworthiness relies on the design of the website (Sillence *et al.* 2006). Lindgaard *et al.* (2006) found that people can judge the visual attractiveness of a website in 50 milliseconds. Sillence *et al.* (2004) report that within 30 seconds people were able to sift and reject health websites which were sales sites or portals. There have been a number of studies that have identified the critical design elements during this early stage (e.g. Briggs *et al.* 2002; Egger 2000; Fogg *et al.* 2001; Stanford *et al.* 2002; Wang and Emurian 2005). Some of the elements found in trustworthy and untrustworthy sites are summarised in Table 9.1.

However, the effectiveness of certain 'trust cues' is somewhat equivocal (Corritore *et al.* 2001). For instance, the impact of trust 'seals' (for instance, TRUSTe) is uncertain, with some studies finding them to be ineffective (e.g. Nielsen *et al.* 2000). Similarly, the impact of photographs on websites has been found to have both a positive impact on trust (Fogg *et al.* 2001; Nielsen *et al.* 2000) and a neutral or negative impact (Riegelsberger and Sasse 2001). People might also adopt different techniques in assessing trust according to their experience of using the Internet and expertise. Stanford *et al.* (2002) reported that experts assessed websites using reputation and their analysis of the information quality, while consumers were more swayed by the attractiveness of the website design.

Linking models of trust to research findings

It is clear that issues central to the definition of risk are closely linked to how trust is conveyed online. As noted earlier, trust is only really an issue

Table 9.1 Elements used for trust evaluation

	Creates trust	Creates mistrust
Design	• Doesn't mix content and advertising. • Contact information, 'real world' feel (e.g. photographs). • Seals of approval (e.g. TRUSTe).	• Adverts. • Small text. • Poor layout and design (too complex or amateur). • Spelling mistakes. • Broken links. • Slow to load.
Content	• Others' viewpoints (reviews, independent assessments). • Simple language. • Privacy, security policies, customer relations information.	• Too much jargon, confusing terminology. • Sales pitch. • Mixes advertising with content.
Relationship management	• Privacy, security policies, customer relations information. • Personalised services, tailored design.	• No information on returns policy. • No attempt to personalise users' experience.

when there is uncertainty or risk. So it is not surprising that trust cues which address risk seem to be effective. For instance, policies on customer returns and complaints, the presence of privacy and security policies, contact information, telephone helplines and cues to a 'real world' presence all serve to address the risk inherent in purchasing from a website. The findings of Jarvenpaa *et al.* (2000) that perceived size and reputation are important also speak to the perceived risk of conducting business online. In an interpersonal setting, risk is represented by uncertainty that the person we are communicating with is who they say they are. Within an interaction, this can be addressed through the use of increased question asking, cross-referencing sources and across time, and so on.

A second set of trust cues relates to the trust dimension of ability or competence. These cues include the absence of spelling mistakes, clear and uncluttered design, the lack of coding errors or broken links, and so on. As a rule of thumb, it would seem sensible to assume that if an e-commerce site is not competent enough to use a spellchecker or design a decent webpage, then this incompetence may well transfer to their fulfilment of your order or data protection policies. Competence in interpersonal interaction can be conveyed in a number of ways, for instance, through reputation systems or rhetorical devices. Within the formation of relationship, competence is most closely aligned with predictability.

The final set of cues relates to the benevolence dimension of trust. For instance, if an advice website mixes advertising with content, the user may well doubt that it truly has their best interests at heart (instead it may be serving the needs of its sponsor). Other cues found to influence trust (e.g. links to other sites) would seem to reinforce the benevolence attribution. Again, this is reflected in interpersonal interaction through the use of rhetorical devices to establish credibility, through empathy and self-disclosure.

Conclusions

This chapter has demonstrated that individuals are able to find ways to trust others and organisations on the Internet. In many instances they have found alternative indicators of trust to the ones they would typically use in FtF settings. While these new trust systems might work to some extent, in the following two chapters we consider whether individuals trust a little too readily in cyberspace and perhaps hand over too much information about themselves.

10 Cyberstalking and harassment

Violating trust

> Angela Westwater was stalked by a man who lived 5,000 miles away on another continent.
>
> The married mother-of-two was horrified to find that her name and personal details had been posted onto a graphically sexual dating site – and that a distant relative living in Florida was responsible.
>
> She told BBC News Online: 'He had superimposed my head onto pictures of naked porn stars, and he had provided a lot of information about me, like my address and telephone number. He also posted a message somewhere else saying that I was his long lost love and that he was desperate for information about my whereabouts.'
>
> (BBC News 1999)

In the previous chapter we talked about the need to trust other people and organisations in our everyday interactions on the Internet. In addition to concerns about being ripped off and lied to online, some individuals have experienced being cyberstalked and cyber-harassed. As this chapter will illustrate, cyberstalking (a more severe form of cyber-harassment) can be as harrowing an experience, if not more so, as traditional offline stalking. Moreover, cyber-harassment is a new form of harassment that is not only problematic with strangers one meets online, but also with people we know (e.g. fellow students or work colleagues).

Offline harassment and stalking

Harassment refers to a gamut of offensive behaviours. The term is typically used in a legal sense to refer to behaviours that are considered to be threatening or disturbing. Hate speech is an example of racial harassment, while making unwanted and persistent sexual advances in the workplace is an example of sexual harassment. A more severe form of harassment is stalking.

It was not until 1990 that the first law was passed which specifically made stalking a crime. The first stalking law was passed in California in response to the stalking and eventual murder of the actor Rebecca Schaeffer. Although this was the first time that stalking was recognised as a crime, as Spitzberg (2002: 261) states:

> This activity of stalking dates to days of antiquity. Obsessive pursuit of another, whether for purposes of romance or revenge, is evident in accounts of both romantic and historical literary traditions (e.g. Kamir, 1995; Lloyd-Goldstein, 1998; Meloy, 1998).

With the advent of the Internet we now have a new crime to deal with – that of cyberstalking. Cases like the one reported at the beginning of this chapter are on the increase. Nonetheless, there is currently no consensus as to how we need to deal with this crime legally as well as socially.

Electronic harassment

Electronic communication can be used to harass in both similar and new ways. Cyber-harassment might occur as a consequence of a romantic relationship gone wrong, or from unwanted romantic and/or sexual attention. It can happen within the workplace or between organisations. As with the offline world, various forms of harassment take place online, including but not limited to sexual and racial harassment. Barak (2005) points out three types of sexual harassment that can take place in cyberspace: gender harassment, unwanted sexual attention and sexual coercion. In addition to the forms of sexual harassment that Barak discusses, individuals might cyber-harass by gaining access to someone's computer, monitoring individual's keystrokes, sending viruses or destroying a person's reputation.

Defining cyberstalking

Stalking also takes place in the cyber-world. This form of stalking has been named cyberstalking. Although legislation is beginning to recognise this form of harassment as a crime, researchers are still currently working on a universal definition for this term. McGrath and Casey (2002), for instance, have argued:

> Stalking is the repeated uninvited monitoring and/or intrusion into the life and activities of a victim that is usually, but not always, undertaken for the purpose of frightening or intimidating the victim or those around the victim . . . Cyberstalking is merely stalking that uses the Internet for information gathering, monitoring, and/or victim contact.
>
> (pp. 88–89)

The problem with McGrath and Casey's definition is that a definition of cyberstalking should not be restricted to the Internet, but should include any electronic communication device (for instance, the text-messaging feature of mobile phones). Moreover, cyberstalking might be accompanied by traditional forms of stalking and harassment. Bocij (2004) offers a more comprehensive definition of cyberstalking:

> A group of behaviors in which an individual, group of individuals, or organization uses information and communications technology to harass another individual, group of individuals, or organization. Such behaviors may include, but are not limited to, the transmission of threats and false accusations, identity theft, damage to data or equipment, computer monitoring, solicitation of minors for sexual purposes, and any form of aggression. Harassment is defined as a course of actions that a reasonable person, in possession of the same information, would think causes another reasonable person to suffer emotional distress.
>
> (p. 14)

Importantly, Bocij's definition is not restricted to the Internet. Additionally, he rightly points out that cyberstalking can be directed at groups or organisations as well as committed by groups or organisations.

Moving the stalking offline

Cyberstalking does not necessarily remain online. Cyberstalking behaviour can potentially initiate online and progress to offline methods of stalking, including all traditional offline stalking behaviours such as the phone, being followed, sending letters, and so forth. In addition, the potential victim might simply be identified online and then stalked offline (Griffiths 2000a).

To give an example of cyberstalking, a classic case is outlined here where the Woodside Literacy Agency stalked Jayne Hitchcock (Bocij 2004; Deirmenjian 1999). When Jayne Hitchcock sent her book proposal to the Woodside Literacy Agency she received a reply complimenting her on her proposal and requesting a reading fee. A few months later postings emerged on Usenet groups warning writers of this company. This prompted writers to test the company's credibility by sending their poorly written manuscripts. They too were complimented on their work and requested to pay a reading fee. When Woodside discovered what was happening, the owner Leonard retaliated by spamming individuals. He then impersonated Hitchcock in various newsgroups and sent messages containing inflammatory comments. In one such message it claimed that Hitchcock was into sadomasochistic practices and provided her phone number. This led to a barrage of phone calls to Hitchcock, which she obviously found harassing. Leonard was arrested in 2000 on charges of conspiracy to commit mail fraud.

Cyberstalking and the law

Some legislation on stalking has been rewritten to include cyberstalking. For example, in South Australia the legislation defines cyberstalking as:

> where stalkers take advantage of information technology either to cause physical or mental harm to the victim, or to cause the victim to feel serious apprehension or fear. Cyberstalking occurs when a person on at least two separate occasions with an intent to cause serious harm, uses the Internet or some other form of electronic communication to publish or transmit offensive material, or communicates with the person, or to others about that person in a manner that could reasonably be expected to arouse apprehension or fear.
>
> (SA Crimes Act 1990)

In a US Attorney General Report (1999), cyberstalking was defined as: 'the use of the Internet, e-mail, or other electronic communications devices to stalk another person'. Interestingly, the England and Wales Protection from Harassment Act 1997 includes neither stalking nor cyberstalking in its definition of harassing behaviour. Instead, it states that:

> A person must not pursue a course of conduct which amounts to the harassment of another person. No intent is required: instead the 'reasonable person' test is used, qualified in the Act by the words 'in possession of the same information'. The offence of causing harassment is unusual in that it is not always necessary to prove that a person actually knew the conduct amounted to harassment. The mental element in harassment is established on proof that the suspect knew or ought to have known that the conduct amounted to harassment (section1(1)). Its effects upon the victim determine whether a course of conduct amounts to 'harassment'. The advantage to this is that any persistent, unwanted behaviour can amount to harassment – permitting police to intervene before behaviour escalates to violence.

Laws that come closer to dealing with cyber-harassment and cyberstalking in the UK include Section 1 of the Malicious Communications Act 1988 which states that it is an offence to send an indecent, offensive or threatening letter, electronic communication or other article to another person, and the Telecommunications Act 1984 which states that it is an offence to send a telephone message which is indecent, offensive or threatening.

Cyber-harassment in the workplace

Cyber-harassment is not just a concern for legislators; it is also a problem that employers need to acknowledge and deal with. Harassment in the workplace can occur on a number of levels. It can be on an interpersonal level and may even lead to more severe harassment such as cyberstalking. It can also occur via a group attack on an individual within an organisation. According to Bocij (2004), an organisation's reputation can be completely destroyed as a consequence of cyber-harassment. He gives an interesting example of where an organisation was stalked by proxy:

> It was alleged that Procter & Gamble had sponsored a web site that encouraged complaints against Amyway. It is alleged that the site featured negative news stories, personal testimonials, and even confidential documents belonging to Amyway. This kind of behaviour can be considered corporate stalking-by-proxy since it involved a company using a third party to harass a competitor.
>
> (Bocij 2004: 143)

Cyber-harassment in the workplace can also take the form of obscene or hate e-mails/text messages that threaten or frighten, or e-mails/text messages that include offensive content such as sexist or racist material. What is unique about this type of workplace harassment, compared to more traditional forms of harassment, is that the harasser is not necessarily a work colleague. For instance, an individual outside of the workplace (either known or not known to the person) might be the harasser. In addition, spam might be considered a form of harassment (e.g. pornographic spam). Spam is an extremely difficult problem to obviate, especially since it is hard to locate the source of the e-mail.

Viewing pornography or pornographic pictures might also be construed by some as a form of sexual harassment. Studies have found that individuals do admit to viewing this pornographic content in the workplace. Elron Software (2001) reported that about one in ten participants stated they had seen fellow workers accessing adult websites. Moreover, one out of three participants stated that they received sexist material via e-mail, and one out of eight said that they received racist material via e-mail. In Whitty's (2004c) research, which she conducted with the company SurfControl, similar concerns arose. In her Australia-wide study, 17 per cent of participants stated that they had been harassed in e-mails in their workplace, while 49 per cent said they had received offensive e-mails. In response to what type of material should be banned in the workplace, a significant proportion of women (67 per cent) compared to men (55 per cent) stated that offensive material such as porn should be banned. Furthermore, women disagreed more strongly than men in their responses to whether workers should be permitted to access sexual material from the web at work. In stark contradiction, in Whitty's same study it was found that one-third of participants believed it was acceptable for workers to discuss sexual matters at work. According to Whitty and Carr (2005b, 2006b) there are three main concerns about these results. First, what kind of sexual details were being discussed?

Second, are these e-mails ever seen by other employees, and if so is this construed as harassment? Third, have there been instances where employees have accidentally sent these e-mails to someone for whom it was not intended?

Cyber-ORI

Spitzberg and his colleagues have focused on romantic harassment and stalking (e.g. Cupach and Spitzberg 1998; Cupach *et al.* 2000; Spitzberg and Cupach 2002, 2003; Spitzberg and Hoobler 2002). They have coined the term 'Obsessional Relational Intrusion' (ORI) to mean 'repeated and unwanted pursuit and invasion of one's sense of physical or symbolic privacy by another person, either stranger or acquaintance, who desires and/ or presumes an intimate relationship' (Cupach and Spitzberg 1998: 234–235). Spitzberg and Hoobler (2002) have contended that 'most stalking is a form of ORI but the two phenomena are not isomorphic' (p. 73). Cupach *et al.* (2000) have argued that ORI is closely related to the legal concept of stalking, except that ORI is broader in meaning. Stalking, they contend, is an 'extreme and severe manifestation of ORI. Stalking involves a pattern of intrusion that a reasonable person would find threatening. Although ORI can be threatening, sometimes it is merely harassing or annoying' (p. 132). These theorists also believe that the motivations for stalking and ORI can be different, in that ORI is motivated by the desire for a relational connection, whereas stalking does not have to be.

Spitzberg and Hoobler (2002) have explored what constitutes cyber-obsessional relational intrusion (cyber-ORI). In their study they identified three types of cyber-obsessional relational pursuit, including *hyperintimacy*, *RL-transference*, and *threat*. They stated that hyperintimacy included sending excessively disclosive messages, tokens of affection, exaggerated messages of affection and pornographic/obscene messages or images. Examples of real life transference (RL-transference) included meeting first online and then threatening the person, meeting the person online and then following them offline, and attempting to disable the person's computer. Finally, examples of threat included sending threatening written messages, sending threatening pictures or images, and sabotaging the individual's private reputation.

In the same study Spitzberg and Hoobler (2002) investigated university students' experiences of cyber-ORI. Of the 235 undergraduate communication students they surveyed, they found that one-third of the respondents reported some form of cyber-based unwanted pursuit. Most of this cyber-ORI was relatively harassing but benign. Nonetheless, some participants had been victimised by some of the more devious types of cyber-ORI. For example, 3 per cent of the sample had had their online persona stolen on at least one occasion. Those more at risk of experiencing cyber-ORI were individuals who were exposed more to cyberspace (e.g. those who more frequently read and participated in chat room discussions and computer-based fantasy games). As Spitzberg and Hoobler (2002) express: 'the more everyday mundane activities a person is exposed to on the World Wide Web, Internet, and cyber-based world of electronic communication, the more at risk the person is for experiencing unwanted pursuit through those very same media' (p. 86).

Coping with cyber-ORI

Spitzberg and Hoobler (2002) conclude from their study:

> the more severe and deviant forms of cyber-pursuit showed little or no relationship to coping responses, suggesting that the objects of such threatening cyber-based activities and of transference of the pursuit from the cyber to the spatial world may nonplus or immobilize victims of pursuit. It may be that such saturation of pursuit disables the victim, creating a feeling that every means of communication and contact is contaminated by the possibility of future unwanted pursuit.
>
> (pp. 86–87)

Interestingly, Spitzberg and Hoobler (2002) have pointed out that some of the available online support for victims of cyberstalking (e.g. online support groups) might not be so helpful. They argue that this is because after experiencing threatening electronic communication this group of individuals might associate any future online communication as a potential threat.

Similarities and differences between online and offline stalking

Meloy (1998) points out that some perpetrators might be drawn more to cyberspace to stalk their victims because of its unique qualities. He argues that 'the Internet allows communication with another person unconstrained by social reality' (p. 11). Similarly, Whitty and Carr (2005b, 2006a) have also argued that harassment online might be more prolific given the nature of this space. For example, because of the lack of obvious and immediate online monitoring, cyberspace might appear to be a more private space. As a consequence individuals might be able to separate themselves more from reality when they communicate in cyberspace. Moreover, if someone is stalking solely through text, asynchronously, arguably they might feel more detached from the situation, thus being less aware of how threatening their harassing communication actually is. Meloy (1998) also contends that 'the absence of sensory-perceptual stimuli from a real person means that fantasy can play an even more expansive role as the genesis of behavior in the stalker' (p. 11).

Using a snowballing sampling method, Bocij (2003) has empirically identified some similarities and differences between online and offline stalking. For instance, he found that contrary to offline stalking, a relatively high proportion of the cyberstalking victims he sampled (42 per cent) reported that they did not know the identity of their harassers. This contrasts dramatically to what is known about offline stalking (McGrath and Casey 2002). Another interesting difference between the two forms of stalking revealed in Bocij's (2003) research was the period of time over which a typical cyberstalking case unfolds. He found that the harassment ranged from two weeks to 38 months. In offline stalking previous research has found that victims tend to be harassed over a much longer period of time than was revealed by Bocij (2003). For example, Sheridan *et al.* (2002) found that almost a third of offline stalking cases lasted for three years or longer. Although it is difficult to generalise Bocij's (2003) results because they were generated from a snowballing technique, nonetheless they do raise some interesting differences between online and offline stalking.

There are of course numerous similarities that ought to be highlighted between online and offline stalking. Bocij (2003) found that cyberstalkers tend to focus on four main activities: issuing threats; harming the victim's reputation; causing damage to data or equipment; and attempting to access confidential information and computer monitoring. He argued that these activities parallel common activities which stalkers engage in offline. For example, Bocij (2003) states that 'attempting to cause damage to data by inserting a computer virus onto the victim's computer system is comparable to the vandalism experienced by some victims of offline stalking'.

Severity of cyberstalking compared to offline stalking

Spitzberg and Hoobler (2002) predict that cyberstalking will increase as a problem before we find ways to obviate this crime. They have argued that 'as access increases, opportunities for manifesting the dark side of human relations in a new medium also increase' (p. 76). They point out that research has identified that a small proportion of the population have been found to be addicted to the Internet (Griffiths 2000b) or are cybersex compulsives (Cooper *et al.* 1999, 2000). These types of people might also be inclined to cyberstalk.

Bocij (2003, 2004) has also pointed out that the harm caused by cyberstalking can be much more severe than any equivalent offline acts. This is especially the case when it comes to attempting to destroy someone's reputation. As Bocij (2003) states: 'This is because information posted to the Internet is available to a huge audience and can remain easily accessible for a great deal of time.' Both individuals' and organisations' reputations have been destroyed in cyberspace. To give an example, there have been websites set up where one can destroy one's ex-partner's reputation: sites like www.formergirlfriends.com/index.php and www.outmyex.com/. On such sites, ex-partners place up naked (and often unflattering) photos of their ex-partners. They also write negative comments about them. Table 10.1 is an

Table 10.1 Extract from a revenge site

My Ex

Tell us what they're TRULY like in bed! Don't hold back!	The bastard had plenty of practice! He should've been better though!
Girls, tell us how BIG it REALLY is!	Looks like a Tic Tac.
Your warning to others about your Ex that they should KNOW!	He is hot I admit, but he's a major dick! All he ever did was talk about how hard he works out and all that bullshit. He is a big liar too! He told me that he was at the bar with his friends and he was sleeping with my best friend!! Skanky ho and major dick! He hangs out with his other dickhead friends at Coyote Ugly and Club Nikita.
Rate Your Ex as an overall Player or Hoochie!	10-Player to the 3rd power and run like hell from him!
Tell us what they were like when you met and how they CHANGED!	Well he was all sweet and sexy sending me nice emails and ecards. About a month into the relationship he was sending them to others!
Is your Ex a LIAR??	D!CKHEAD NEVER TOLD THE TRUTH!
Is your Ex a CHEATER??	Hell yes! Caught that D!CKHEAD CHEATING!

extract from outmyex.com, which demonstrates one woman's thoughts about her ex-boyfriend.

It is noteworthy that the Internet is set up in such a way as to make it easy for individuals to monitor others. If one is connected to software such as IM or Skype those linked up to the contact can tell when one is logged in. Google has made it much easier for people to track down their ex-partners and even spy on their activities. Google Earth provides fairly clear pictures of people's houses and their backyards. Online daters have been found to regularly check up on their potential dates' activities to see how much they are playing the field (Whitty and Carr 2006a). Software has been created to check on your partner's online activities – down to knowing every keystroke they make. As Spytech Online (n.d.) reports:

> Our monitoring software can quickly detect and give you the evidence you need to prove that your spouse is remaining faithful to you – or cheating on you. Our spy software tools, such as *SpyAgent* and *Realtime-Spy*, can operate in total stealth – defeating the built in Windows task manager and popular spyware detection tools. These abilities mean you will not have to worry about your spouse discovering you are monitoring them – and even if you inform them they will

still not be able to tell how. Logs can even be stored in an encrypted format, so they can only be viewed with our software.

Given the ease with which one can monitor others without apparently being caught out, then Spitzberg and Hoobler (2002) are probably correct in saying that the problem of cyberstalking will continue to increase over time.

Dealing with cyber-harassment

Although harassment online can have as serious an impact on the individual being harassed as traditional harassment, our places of work, our laws (only a few jurisdictions consider cyberstalking, for instance, in their legislation) and police authorities are not dealing adequately with this crime. Workplaces need to have policies to ensure individuals are not harassed in this way and to make those policies transparent. Not only do countries and states need to consider this form of harassment in their legislation, but there is also an urgent need to consider how to deal with this crime on an international scale (given that perpetrator and victim can be in a different countries). Moreover, as a society we need to increase public awareness of this crime and to educate the public on how to deal with it and to know what support is available. Currently, there are web pages dedicated to supporting victims of cyberstalking. Some of those organisations that have set up support web pages include: Working to Halt Online Abuse, CyberAngels and WiredSafety. CyberAngels, for instance, defines cyberstalking, gives tips on how to respond to the cyberstalker and informs the victim on the potential severity of the crime and the importance of reporting it to the police. WiredSafety, in addition, focuses on specific places online such as blogs and online datings and tailors safety tips in using each of these sites.

Conclusions

Much empirical work still needs to be carried out on the topic of cyber-harassment and cyberstalking. Moreover, in the future cyberstalking will need to be considered more on an international scale. As discussed in this chapter, there is neither a universal definition for this crime nor adequate laws to deal with it on an international level. Workplaces will need to consider more effective ways to protect their organisations as well as their employees. While online sites might be of a certain amount of assistance to some victims of this crime, this is clearly not enough – especially for those victims who have become too afraid to use the Internet as a consequence of experiencing cyber-harassment.

11 Surveillance, privacy and trust

Although it can be exaggerated, the use of computers and telecommunications undoubtedly helps hasten both the growth and the integration of surveillance. Indeed, the use of similar kinds of technical systems and software, plus the decisive shift toward a consumer phase of capitalism, meant that in the later part of the twentieth century a subtle transformation occurred. The surveillance state expanded to become the surveillance society.

(Lyon 2003: 94)

There is no doubt that technology and how we use it changes at an ever-increasing pace. We have detailed in this book instances where trust has broken down online – leading to heartache and sometimes to the loss of large sums of money. As Chapter 9 demonstrated, individuals do, to some extent, trust others and organisations on the Internet. As we shall demonstrate in this chapter, perhaps they do this too readily. Considerations of surveillance versus privacy are crucial notions that we need to examine more seriously on both an individual and societal level.

The nature of privacy

You have zero privacy anyway . . . Get over it.

(McNealy 1999)

It has long been argued that new communication technology poses an unprecedented threat to people's privacy. As we rely increasingly on it in our daily lives, so we also leave a 'data footprint' that allows sophisticated data mining techniques to open our private lives to scrutiny. Cheap storage and processing of data, when combined with an ever-increasing amount of information collected in the name of authentication, personalisation and convenience, means that for most people large amounts of personal information are stored about who they are and how they live their lives.

There are numerous cases of the clash between privacy and new technology – how these technologies allow intrusions into private, enclosed spaces, eroding the distinction between public and private space and therefore compromising the very idea of private space. Advances in technology and increased use of the Internet have changed the ways in which information is gathered and used. A wide variety of information data is now collected with increasing frequency and in different contexts, making individuals become ever more transparent. The costs of obtaining and analysing this are also decreasing with the advances in technology. However, the value of the information collected is increasing:

> At no time have privacy issues taken on greater significance than in recent years, as technological developments have led to the emergence of an 'information society' capable of gathering, storing and disseminating increasing amounts of data about individuals.
>
> (Schatz Byford 1996: 1)

There are a number of specific threats to online privacy. For example, the impact of 'ubiquitous' computing (Weiser 1988) means that we leave data footprints in many areas of our lives that were previously considered 'offline'. The extremely rapid development of computing power, in terms of greater processing speed, increased storage capacity, wider communication connectivity and lower machine size, all impact on privacy (Sparck-Jones 2003). These rapid advances mean that information can be efficiently and cheaply collected, stored and exchanged – even data which may be deemed sensitive by the individuals concerned. This 'privacy cost' of new technology applies both to services we choose to use and to the generalised collection and storage of data from our daily lives.

What is privacy?

When we talk about privacy, we often think of unauthorised or unwarranted access to personal information – for instance, someone reading others' e-mails, accessing their bank accounts or medical records or taking unwanted photographs of them. Indeed, many approaches to understanding privacy deal almost exclusively with the access of information. However, definitions based solely on illegitimate access to information are not sufficient. It is possible to infringe someone's privacy without gaining new information; for instance, video filming your neighbours in their garden will most likely violate their privacy, but it is unlikely that new information is gained.

In a legal context, privacy is largely synonymous with a 'right to be let alone' (Warren and Brandeis 1890). However, others have argued that privacy is only the right to prevent the disclosure of personal information. For instance, Westin (1967) defines privacy as 'the claim of individuals, groups, or institutions to determine for themselves when, how and to what extent information about them is communicated to others' (p. 7). Westin (1967) proposes four main functions of privacy: *personal autonomy* applies to the need for the development of individuality and the avoidance of manipulation by others; *emotional release* refers to the need for opportunities to relax and escape from the tensions of everyday life in order to support healthy functioning; *self-evaluation* is the application of individuality on to events and the integration of experience into meaningful patterns; and *limited and protected communication* refers to both the sharing of personal information with trusted others and the setting of interpersonal boundaries.

Altman (1975) incorporates both social and environmental psychology in understanding the nature of privacy. He defines privacy as 'the selective control of access to the self' (p. 24) and believes that privacy is achieved through the regulation of social interaction, which can in turn provide us with feedback on our ability to deal with the world, and ultimately affect our definition of self.

The definition of privacy is further complicated because it is both a preference and a state (Margulis 2003); that is, people can 'have' privacy, or they can desire privacy. Privacy is also dynamic in that it serves to regulate social interaction (Altman 1975; Derlega and Chaikin 1977), while at the same time it can highlight uneven power relations (Derlega and Chaikin 1977), be used to signify trust (Altman 1975), or begin a process of reciprocation (Archer 1976). It is possible that people might trade one form of privacy for another (Joinson and Paine 2007).

Many researchers have referred to the difficulties involved in trying to produce a definition (e.g. Burgoon *et al.* 1989) and, despite various attempts to create a synthesis of existing literature (e.g. Parent 1983; Schoeman 1984), a unified and simple account of privacy has yet to emerge. Although there is no unitary concept of privacy, it is clear that both individuals and society attach a level of importance to it. For example, Ingham (1978) states that 'man, we are repeatedly told is a social animal, and yet he constantly seeks to achieve a state of privacy' (p. 45).

Like trust, the highly complex nature of privacy has resulted in an alternative way of defining it – through its various dimensions. Burgoon *et al.* (1989) distinguish four dimensions of privacy and define it using these dimensions: 'the ability to control and limit physical, interactional, psychological and informational access to the self or one's group' (Burgoon *et al.* 1989: 132). DeCew (1997), one of those who argues for a multidimensional approach to understanding privacy, distinguishes three dimensions: informational; accessibility; and expressive.

Informational privacy

Informational privacy includes personal information, for example, personal lifestyle, finances, medical history and academic achievement. It may be viewed by an individual as information not to be divulged and to be guarded by any recipients of that information. The protection of informational privacy shields individuals from intrusions as well as the fear of threats of intrusions, and it also affords them control in deciding who has access to the information and for what purposes. In the UK, the Data Protection Act (DPA) covers informational privacy in that it deals with the collection and sharing of personal information (including student examination scores).

Accessibility privacy

Accessibility privacy refers to physical or sensory access to a person. In this activity, accessibility refers to this type of privacy, rather than relating to the use of technology by disabled people. According to DeCew (1997), accessibility privacy covers both physical proximity and observation. So, we have accessibility privacy when we wish to maintain physical distance from others (for instance, if we wish to study in an empty, quiet room), and we lose it when watched by CCTV. Accessibility privacy also covers access through other senses (e.g. sight or hearing), in particular others' surveillance of aspects of our lives we wish to engage in in seclusion. According to DeCew, it 'allows individuals to control decisions about who has physical access to their persons through sense perception, observation, or bodily contact' (pp. 76–77).

Expressive privacy

Expressive privacy 'protects a realm for expressing one's self-identity or personhood through speech or activity. It protects the ability to decide to continue or to modify one's behaviour when the activity in question helps define oneself as a person, shielded from interference, pressure and coercion from government or from other individuals' (DeCew 1997: 77). In this way, expressive privacy restricts external social control over choices about lifestyle, and improves internal control over self-expression and the ability to build interpersonal relationships. This aspect of privacy 'prevents interference, pressures to conform, ridicule, punishment . . . it functions to promote liberty of action' (Gavison 1980: 448).

Central to understanding privacy is people's desire to keep personal information out of the hands of others, and to maintain their ability to connect with others without interference. This desire has also been called *privacy concern* (Westin 1967). However, it is not clear how privacy concerns actually link to behaviour online. There is evidence that although many Internet users express privacy-protectionist attitudes, this rarely translates to their actual behaviour (Jupiter Research 2002; Pew Internet and American Life Project 2001). For instance, Spiekermann *et al.* (2001) measured the privacy preferences of 171 users and observed their behaviour on a mock e-commerce site. On this site, the users were 'helped' by a 'bot (short for an automated agent or 'robot') that asked a number of purchase-related questions of differing levels of intrusiveness. They found very little evidence that privacy preferences were related to people's actual behaviour in response to the 'bots questions. The failure of various privacy enhancing technologies in the marketplace also suggests a disjunction between people's stated attitudes and their actual actions to protect their privacy (Acquisti and Grossklags 2003).

Privacy and the Internet

As we have seen earlier, the Internet and IT advances in general pose a unique challenge to personal privacy. The rapid advances in networking, processing and storage mean that information can be efficiently and cheaply collected, stored and exchanged – even data which may be deemed sensitive by the individuals concerned. Information that is drawn from the physical world is harboured in electronic databases, which give these records the permanence, malleability and transportability that has become the trademark of technology. As such, massive databases and Internet records of information about individual financial and credit history, medical records, purchases, and so on exist. Sparck-Jones (2003) labels a number of specific properties of the information collected which have consequences for privacy:

- *Permanence* – once recorded, information rarely disappears. As such, fine-grained, searchable, persistent data exist on individuals and there are sophisticated, cheap data-mining devices that can be used to analyse this information.
- *Volume* – the ease with which information is now recorded using technology results in huge data sets. Furthermore, storage is cheap, therefore large volumes of information sets can exist indefinitely.
- *Invisibility* – all information collected seems to exist within an opaque system and so any information collected may not be 'visible' to those to whom it relates. Even if information collected is available to a person, they may not be able to interpret it due to the use of incomprehensible coding.
- *Neutrality* – the ease with which information can be collected means that any qualifying information may be lost. So information may be absorbed regardless of its metadata; that is, there are no distinctions between intimate, sensitive information and non-sensitive information.
- *Accessibility* – there are a number of tools for accessing information, meaning that any information collected can possibly be read by any number of people. The ease with which information can be copied, transferred, integrated and multiplied electronically further increases this accessibility.
- *Assembly* – there are many effective tools for searching for, assembling and reorganising information from many quite separate sources.

- *Remoteness* – information collected is usually both physically and logically away from the users to whom it refers. However, this information can be accessed and used by people whom the user does not know.

Each of the above features affects privacy uniquely and in combination with other threats. Although massive data collection and storage is possible in many environments, the very structure of the Internet and its additional feature of connectivity further exacerbate the online privacy problem. The Internet allows for interactive two-way communication and is woven into people's lives in a more intimate way than some other media as it connects people with places and people with people. Accordingly, it poses unique information privacy threats that differ from issues previously addressed by research (e.g. Smith *et al.* 1996), therefore making information collection, sharing, and so on even easier.

There are also *benefits* to the technological advances described, such as personalised services, convenience and efficiency. In this way, the collection of personal information can be considered a 'double edged sword' (Malhotra *et al.* 2004). Users can trade off providing valuable information about themselves to take advantage of benefits; for example, providing personal details and credit card information in order to have the convenience of completing an online transaction. Jupiter Research (2002) has found evidence that even privacy concerned individuals are willing to trade off privacy for convenience, or to bargain the release of very personal information in exchange for relatively small rewards. However, consumer concern over disclosing personal information is growing as they realised that data about their Internet behaviours is being collected without their knowledge and agreement. These privacy concerns can ultimately reduce the personalisation benefits that companies can deliver to consumers. The question is whether the benefits of the advances in technology and the use of the Internet are diminished by endangering privacy.

Spying on our friends and family

When we send an e-mail to a close family member or chat with a friend on Instant Messenger we might assume we are engaging in a private discourse. However, is this actually the case? Unfortunately, we cannot assume that we have complete privacy online. There are many ways in which individuals can and often do monitor people's online interactions.

Software to spy

There are numerous software packages available that monitor and record other people's online activities, including viewing and recording people's e-mails, chat messages, websites visited, as well as the monitoring and recording keystrokes, and even individuals' passwords. For example, 007 Spy Software (n.d.) advertises as follows:

> 007 Spy Software is a stealthy computer monitoring software which allows you to secretly record all activities of computer users and automatically deliver logs to you via Email or FTP, including all areas of the system such as email sent, Web sites visited, every keystroke (including login/password of ICQ, MSN, AOL, AIM, and Yahoo Messenger or Webmail), file operations, online chat conversation, and take screen snapshots at set intervals just like a surveillance camera directly points at the computer monitor.

People advertising such software promote it as a way for employers to monitor their employees, as well as for individuals to check on family members in the home, including one's children or even one's spouse. For example, Wiretap Professional (n.d.) has the following to say about their software:

> How Can You Use Wiretap?
>
> Whether you are an employer in the work place or you are a concerned parent at home, reliable, secure, PC Activity and Internet Monitoring solution is a click away.
>
> You're an Employer > On the Job
>
> - Monitor employee activity on office computers.
> - Spy Software can prevent theft of valuable company data.
> - Document illegal or unethical activity by using Wiretap's log files.
> - Spy Software can detect unwanted activity before it becomes a problem or liability.
> - Enforce existing company policies and rules.
> - Insure your company's IT integrity by using Wiretap spy software as a preventative tool.
>
> You're a Parent > In the Home
>
> - Keep track of your children's activity. Spy software lets you see exactly where they go on the web.
> - Instant Message monitoring and Email Sniffing allows you to stay on top of who your child is communicating with! Keep them safe from predators who take advantage of children.
> - Keep tabs on an untrustworthy spouse! Got an inkling something is up? Now you can be sure, spy software lets you investigate easily.
> - Watch and track what roommates and others who have access to your PC do while you're away.

- Log your own activities and communications for your own reference.
- Logs are often invaluable when trying to remember important details about your PC activity.

As outlined in the previous chapter the software Spytech online (n.d.) advertises their spy software as a way to catch out a cheating spouse.

To Google

In addition to purchasing software to spy on others' activities online, one can monitor people's lives by seeking out information about them. 'To Google' someone has become a common verb to describe seeking out information about another person online. This might be a long-lost love, lost friends, or even ourselves to see what is being said about us online. Websites are set up to encourage individuals to provide information about others for others' use. For example, the authors of the website RateMyProfessor (n.d.) advertise their site thus:

> Professors Beware: Students Are Doing the Grading, Announces RateMyProfessors.com

> Menlo Park, CA – October 5, 2005 – Students have turned the tables on their professors at RateMyProfessors.com (http://www.ratemypro-fessors.com), the Internet's largest listing of college professor ratings. The free website offers a public review (and sometimes a public flog-ging) of university professors from across the United States, Canada and Ireland. . . .
> 'Every semester, millions of students use the site to help plan their class schedules, and improve the quality of their educations,' says the site's president and founder, John Swapceinski. 'When word of the website gets out at a university, the ratings grow like wildfire and students really begin to benefit from the information.'
> RateMyProfessors allows students to anonymously rate their professors in each of three categories: Helpfulness, Clarity, and Easi-ness. Now, students can see who the hottest professors are at their school, as well as read the top 15 funniest ratings, like rating number 5: 'He will destroy you like an academic ninja.'

Who are people monitoring online and what information are they looking for?

Mark Andrejevic (2006), in an international study, has found that out of his sample of 549 participants an impressive 75 per cent admitted to having used the Internet to search for information about others. This suggests that

Table 11.1 Type of information participants were
seeking out about others online

What they looked for	Frequency (per cent)
Photos	299 (55)
Contact information	276 (50)
Personal information	246 (45)
Location	193 (35)
Professional activity	96 (18)
Information about their family and friends	82 (15)
Criminal records	70 (13)
Educational background	67 (12)
Legal records	62 (11)
Marital relationship history	42 (8)
Employment history	26 (5)
Information on infidelity	19 (4)

the monitoring of others, at least in cyberspace, is common practice. However, it is noteworthy that the majority of participants were between the ages of 18 and 24 years. It might be that this group of individuals are more Internet savvy. Moreover, this group of participants, who have grown up with reality television, might be more likely to believe that surveillance is an acceptable activity.

Participants in his study claimed to have monitored a range of people in their lives including: friends (67 per cent); significant others (36 per cent); former friends (33 per cent); new acquaintances (30 per cent); former significant others (28 per cent); potential dates (25 per cent); parents (24 per cent); employers (23 per cent); siblings (20 per cent); co-workers (15 per cent); neighbours (9 per cent). The participants stated that they used the following devices to gather information about these people: search engines such as Google (67 per cent); e-mail (20 per cent); Friendster and MySpace (20 per cent); and free web background checks (10 per cent).

The type of information that Andrejevic's participants were seeking out is presented in Table 11.1. Interestingly, despite the number of software packages available to check on one's spouse's fidelity, only 4 per cent mentioned seeking out such information. The most popular method to seek out information about others was via IM or chat (43 per cent) and mobile phones (25 per cent). Only 2 per cent of participants opted to use keystroke monitoring. Of further interest is that 41 per cent of the participants admitted to using the Internet to gather background information about themselves.

Is all this online monitoring a good thing?

Lyon (2003) warns us to consider the social implications of surveillance carried out by computer systems. He points out that the type of computer surveillance carried out prior to the Internet was quite different. This type of surveillance focused on specific data and on particular activities. Now that the Internet has become part of our everyday lives, our surveillance activities have also become a part them. As Lyon (2003) explains:

> The surveillance situation altered once it became possible to extend the 'gaze' from national state and capitalist corporation record-keeping and monitoring to include all kinds of everyday transactions. The records of Mohammed Atta, on CCTV tapes and digital logs, were collected not because he was doing anything unusual or deviant. Just the opposite. Data-gathering is routine, generalized, and distributed across almost every sphere of life.
>
> (pp. 96–97)

Others have questioned whether all surveillance is an acceptable activity, especially when it comes to the workplace (Greenfield and Davis 2002; Kidwell and Bennett 1994; Whitty 2004b). Those who support workplace online surveillance are likely to argue that it is necessary to ensure employees are not 'cyberslacking' or using the companies' resources for inappropriate activities in the workplace, such as downloading pornography. Those who have argued strongly against this form of monitoring parallel the Internet with other forms of communication in the workplace, such as the telephone (Fisher 2002). They have highlighted that the telephone has traditionally been accepted as a mode of communication used for private purposes. Given this, the Internet should also be acceptable for private purposes in the workplace, such as a quick e-mail to one's loved one, or to organise a social gathering with friends. Others have also argued that employees might interpret employers' monitoring of their online activities as a breach of trust (Whitty 2004b).

Whitty (2004b) surveyed 524 Australians about their views on workplace surveillance. Participants had mixed opinions as to what aspects of the Internet ought to be monitored and whether filtering software should be used by employers. In the main, participants felt that they ought to be allowed to use the Internet at work for non-work related activities, some of which included personal e-mails, surfing for information such as news and politics, entertainment, banking, education, research, job search, porn, chat rooms and jokes. Nonetheless, they still maintained that some of their activities ought to be monitored. For example, 37 per cent of participants stated that the Internet at work should be monitored for the downloading or viewing of offensive material such as porn, discriminating or criminal material.

Others have contended that not only should we be concerned with what our current employers are monitoring us for, but also what kinds of information about ourselves prospective employers might be finding out about us. In a newspaper article, Weiss (2006) warns her readers that an increasing number of employers are 'googling' potential employees. Weiss (2006) makes the point that it might not be information which we have ourselves placed online, but rather information others have written about us:

> Sure, you may not have intentionally posted something controversial about yourself online, but from blogs to dating profiles, the Web has become a place where people air dirty laundry without a thought, making it a dangerous place to mix business with pleasure.
>
> (Weiss 2006)

Of course not only are people 'googling' potential employees, but they are also checking out their social networking profiles. Given that on these sites individuals are typically linked up to their 'offline' friends who are aware of their offline activities, then comments left on a person's site and tagged photographs are likely to give a 'real' picture of what they are like in everyday situations. Comments about their weekend activities (e.g. excessive drinking or who they managed to 'pull') are often not written with a larger audience in mind. Nonetheless this information can often be accessed by a larger audience such as a potential employer. The classic case reported in the media was where Oxford university students were caught out by the university for a prank that they bragged about on Facebook. It had never crossed the students' minds that their lecturers might check out their online profiles (which they obviously only intended for their friends to see) for evidence that might incriminate them (BBC News 2007).

Privacy, trust and online behaviour

When we begin to think about how privacy links to behaviour, we need to distinguish between privacy dispositions and a state of privacy (Paine *et al.* 2006), as well as taking into account related factors like trust. It would seem sensible to argue (as many have) that the impact of privacy on behaviour is mediated by trust in the other partner/organisation. For instance, Malhotra *et al.* (2004) examined the links between people's Internet information privacy concerns and their related behavioural intentions. They found that the effect of privacy concerns on behavioural intentions was mediated by trust. Similarly, Chellappa and Sin (2005) studied consumers' intent to use personalisation services. They found that this intent was influenced by both trust and concern for privacy. Metzger (2004) set up a fake e-commerce site and found a link between privacy concern and self-disclosure mediated by trust. The conclusion would seem to be that lack of privacy is only really important when there is no trust in the recipient of your personal information. If you trust the person, then privacy is less important. In the final chapter of this book we consider the links between privacy and trust in more detail.

Conclusions

The Internet and privacy is paradoxical. Just as anonymity online enables both honesty and deceit, so new technology both threatens and provides opportunities for privacy. By adopting a multidimensional approach to privacy, it is possible that the same environments – say a chat site – can encourage expressive privacy while also reducing informational privacy (and to a degree accessibility). To fully understand the links between privacy, trust and online behaviour, we need to ask not just 'Is person X anonymous?', but also 'To whom are they anonymous, and to whom are they known?'

12 Developing trust in online counselling

Trust online is obviously an important concern for psychologists who opt to counsel their clients on the Internet. Online counselling is no longer a therapy that will take place in the future but rather is a form of therapy currently being adopted by clients and therapists around the world. Online counselling has been defined by Manhal-Baugus (2001) as 'the process of interacting with a therapist online in ongoing conversations over time when the client and counsellor are in separate or remote locations and utilize electronic means to communicate with each other' (p. 551). Although this definition might appear fairly straightforward, as will become evident in this chapter, there is a variety of ways in which online counselling might be conducted.

Origins of online counselling

Online counselling, also referred to as e-therapy, has been around since the origins of the Internet. Some psychologists will go so far as to argue that 'one can trace e-therapy's roots all the way back to a time when researchers first envisioned uses of computers that went beyond simple number-crunching' (Grohol 2004: 51). For instance, while the Internet was being created, in the 1960s, Weizenbaum developed an interactive program that became known as ELIZA. ELIZA is a program that allows individuals to communicate with it without needing to have any knowledge of computer language. Weizenbaum named this program ELIZA after the character of Eliza Doolittle in the play *Pygmalion* and the musical *My Fair Lady*. The program was designed to appear as if a proper conversation was taking place. Certain words and phrases were programmed to trigger seemingly appropriate responses. The program appeared very human-like – with a semblance to 'Rogerian' psychoanalysis, where the therapist asks questions based purely on what the patient says. Weizenbaum, however, did not believe that ELIZA could one day be used as a substitute for a real-world therapist.

Not everyone agreed with Weizenbaum's pessimism. For instance, his colleague Colby, who also worked with Weizanbaum on ELIZA, believed that such programs had potential for psychotherapy and counselling applications (Grohol 2004). Colby went on to create PARRY, which was a program that simulated a client in therapy who exhibited paranoid behaviour. PARRY was subjected to the Turing test (a term used to describe whether one can determine if the respondent is a real person or a computer program). The Turing test revealed that scientists and psychiatrists did no better than chance in distinguishing PARRY from real clients (Grohol 2004).

Grohol (2004) points out that 'these programs illustrated some of the very first social uses for computers and demonstrated that people would willingly engage in text-based communication for therapeutic purposes' (p. 53). The self-help groups that started sprouting up online during the early stages of the Internet could also be interpreted as people's desire and willingness to engage in text-based therapy. Online counselling later on became more formalised by professionals who were willing to provide free counselling online. Some of the pioneers of online counselling services included John Grohol and Ivan Goldberg (Grohol 2004). In 1994 the Samaritans set up the first e-mail address for individuals contemplating suicide to contact free of charge.

During the dot.com period of the 1990s, psychologists, entrepreneurs, and the like began to realise the potential of earning a good income from using computers to help people. Like many dot.com enterprises, many of these online services failed. Grohol (2004) reports that here2listen.com is a good example of a dot.com gone wrong:

> Co-funded by Gunny Cho, a former international lawyer, and Don Sheu in June 1999, the company boasted an advisory board of renowned psychology experts. Its advisory board included well-respected university professors, such as Larry Beutler from the University of California, Peter Kramer, well-known author of Listening to Prozac, and Philip G. Zimbardo, the president of the American Psychological Association in 2002. . . . without warning or prenotification to its clients or therapists, here2listen.com shuttered its doors in late 2001 . . . Here2listen.com's failure might be related to its infrastructure and development costs, salaries, and policy of paying freelance writers for articles.
>
> (Grohol 2004: 63–64)

Online counselling today

Although online counselling does not reap huge monetary rewards for practitioners, in current times some psychologists, psychiatrists and counsellors worldwide are conducting counselling sessions in cyberspace. It is, however, noteworthy that the proportion of professionals who are willing to utilise the Internet for counselling is still relatively small. VandenBos and

Williams (2000) reported that the current use of online counselling by psychologists associated with the American Psychological Association ranges from 2 per cent for online psychotherapy to 15 per cent for the use of faxes and e-mail to conduct psychological assessments.

Clients are also not embracing this new form of therapy. It has been found that only 10 per cent of Americans would be very or extremely likely to engage in online therapy (Harris Interactive 2004). Even when presented with a less expensive alternative to traditional therapy only 22 per cent of Americans (with a history of treatment) report they would consider telephone or Internet therapy (Harris Interactive 2004). Research has also found that university students have less positive attitudes toward e-therapy than toward traditional FtF counselling (Rochlen *et al.* 2004).

Defining online counselling

e-Therapy can be carried out in a number of online spaces or might be used in conjunction with FtF counselling. For instance, e-therapy has been conducted via e-mail, Instant Messaging, videoconferencing (which includes audio and visual information) and chat rooms. Group therapy can also be conducted online (Sander 1996). In Japan there is a short-message texting based counselling service provided through employee assistance plans (EAPs: Fenichel 2004). Information websites have also sprouted across the Internet providing detailed information about a range of psychological and physical problems. What is unique about online counselling compared to FtF counselling is that it is typically conducted in the absence of traditional non-verbal cues. In cyberspace, one also has less sense of social presence. In addition, Zelvin and Speyer (2004) claim that 'the boundaries between clinician and client are not quite the same as in f2f [face-to-face] practice. Clients tend to be proactive in searching for references to the therapist, sometimes even before beginning treatment' (p. 173).

Online counselling can be conducted in a variety of ways. It can be conducted asynchronously (e.g. e-mail) or synchronously (e.g. IM). It can be conducted solely through text or it might be conducted using pictures (e.g. avatars, photos) or video (e.g. webcams). Online therapy can be conducted with individual clients or with groups of individuals. Each of the different forms of online counselling has its strengths and weaknesses.

Benefits

Cyberspace presents many individuals with access to services they would otherwise never or could never reach (e.g. the socially shy, isolated or physically challenged). In reference to group therapy, Bellafiore *et al.* (2004) have stated:

The Internet has the advantage of bringing people together, while allowing them to remain in their homes. Online group therapy offers a practical, cost-effective option. It maintains privacy and may serve to diminish social isolation, anxiety, and depression.

(p. 199)

Benefits of online counselling include convenience, access and numerous links to multimedia informative sources. As Fenichel (2004) has pointed out: 'Some relish the opportunities for anonymity, to be creative, to try on new personas and new behaviors, or to find supportive environments as an alternative to "real-life" situations that may be dysfunctional, stressful, or simply boring' (p. 7).

Some researchers contend that 'when individuals write about emotional experiences, significant physical and mental health improvements follow' (Pennebaker 1997: 162). Pennebaker (1997) explains that writing about upsetting experiences can be painful during the days one is writing. Nonetheless, the long-term effects of writing about emotional topics can include improvements in mood, well-being, grades and one's immune system. Given that online counselling via e-mail, IM and chat requires writing, one might surmise that this form of therapy ought to be effective. Wright and Chung (2001), from their review of the literature, have argued that writing is beneficial for those who perceive themselves as powerless, who are not using their first language in FtF counselling, who feel more inhibited, who feel the need to disclose stressful or traumatic events and those who are at particular life stages (e.g. adolescents). Researchers and counsellors have reported that some individuals 'prefer writing as a way to express themselves. They take delight in words, sentence structure, and the creative opportunity to subtly craft exactly how they wish to articulate their thoughts and moods' (Suler 2004b: 20). Hence, one of the strengths of online counselling is that it presents individuals with a unique opportunity to express themselves in ways that can potentially lead to improvements in well-being.

It has been well documented that individuals can feel less inhibited in cyberspace. Suler (2004a) has named this the 'disinhibition effect'. Online therapy (especially when the individual remains anonymous and is interacting in text only) should theoretically enable the client to feel better able to express themselves more openly.

Suler (2004b) has argued that one of the benefits of online counselling is that it provides clients with a 'zone of reflection'. This he believes is more likely the case with asynchronous online therapy such as e-mail. With asynchronous communication one has time to consider a response. As Suler (2004b) states:

You have time to think, evaluate, and compose your reply. This *zone of reflection* comes in very handy for those awkward or emotional situations in a relationship. Some people take advantage of this zone. Others, perhaps acting more spontaneously or at times impulsively, do not.

(p. 25)

Another advantage of asynchronous forms of online therapy is that the client does not have to schedule appointments, but instead can engage in therapy when they find the time. In addition, it provides the convenience of replying when the client is ready (Suler 2004c).

Suler (2004b) believes that synchronous communication also has its benefits. It allows one to schedule meetings, have a greater sense of social presence, interact more spontaneously (and therefore be less censored), and witness pauses in conversations which can give more meaning to the interaction:

> People may be more spontaneous, revealing, uncensored in their self-disclosures. Pauses in the conversation, coming late to a session, and no-shows are not lost as temporal cues that reveal important psychological meanings.

(p. 28)

Whether conducting online therapy via e-mail, chat or IM, one is able to save a permanent record of the session. This is a benefit for the client and the therapist – as both are able to monitor the client's progression more easily than with FtF sessions.

Drawbacks

Online therapy is not the most appropriate modality for every client or every therapist. As Zelvin and Speyer (2004) have expressed: 'Not every competent clinician is a good candidate for online practice. Nor should every client with a computer be encouraged to engage in treatment online' (p. 164). Stofle (2002) makes the point that a therapist who is competent FtF is not necessarily competent online.

Despite the many benefits e-therapy has to offer, there are certain drawbacks to this form of therapy that we also need to consider. Some of these might include the lack of non-verbal cues (making it difficult to express and interpret emotions), misreading of cues, time delays and technological glitches. Although we have noted the therapeutic benefits that writing has to offer, not every client feels comfortable expressing themselves through writing. Suler has noted that the ability to express oneself in writing varies between individuals: 'People who hate to write, or are poor typists, probably will not be drawn to text-based therapy' (Suler 2004b: 20).

Although there are many benefits to be gained from engaging in asynchronous forms of online counselling, there are problems that also need to be highlighted. As Suler (2004c) points out, because there is no appointment the professional boundaries might be blurred. Given the lack of appointments a client might feel less committed and in turn may feel that their therapist is less committed. There is also less chance for individuals to be spontaneous and having less notable pauses in a conversation can be a disadvantage for both therapists and clients.

The disadvantages of synchronous online sessions are also worthy of note. There is the inconvenience of scheduling a meeting, less chance for reflection, and therapy might be perceived by the client as only taking place during the allocated time slot (Suler 2004c). Furthermore, as Suler (2004b) notes, 'the zone of reflection diminishes. Clients may lose the opportunity to compose their message, to say exactly what they want to say' (p. 28).

Is online counselling effective?

Given the pros and cons of online therapy, it is important for researchers to assess the effectiveness of this form of therapy. Only a few researchers have actually examined its effectiveness. Nonetheless, the growing evidence seems to suggest that some forms of online therapy for some clients can be effective in reducing clients' presenting problems. There is anecdotal evidence provided by counsellors that suggests that online counselling has its uses. For example, Yager (2001) found that it was helpful to use e-mail in conjunction with FtF therapy with his anorexia nervosa clients. He found that allowing clients to use e-mail in between sessions enabled them to write and send messages when inspiration struck. He also believed that it reduced the emotional burden on clients and that e-mail made it easier for them to self-disclose. Perhaps this is especially the case for individuals with anorexia nervosa who tend to be shy and socially phobic.

In more scientific research, Cohen and Kerr (1998) assigned 24 undergraduate students to either a FtF counselling session or a computer mediated counselling (CMC) session. Those in the CMC treatment group were counselled through synchronous chat. They found that clients reported significant decreases in anxiety in both modes of treatment, but there was no difference in level of change between the two modes.

Lange *et al.* (2001) randomly assigned 25 college students who were experiencing post-traumatic stress to either a CMC treatment group or a wait-list control group. The treatment group were expected to engage in 45-minute writing exercises twice a week. Halfway through the session clinical psychology graduate students responded to the clients' writing, providing feedback on their progress and instructions on how to proceed. The results revealed that those in the treatment group showed larger reductions in post-traumatic stress symptoms compared to the control group.

Day and Schneider (2002) randomly assigned 80 clients to three modes of psychotherapy: FtF, videoconference and two-way audio. The control group was a wait-list group. These clients presented a range of problems, including weight issues, relationship issues and personality disorders. After completing five sessions, clients in all of the treatment groups reported less severe target complaints and higher 'global assessment of functioning'. This was not the case for the control group. In addition, Day and Schneider (2002) found no significant differences between each of the treatment groups.

Hopps *et al.* (2003) found evidence to support the utility of cognitive behavioural therapy (CBT) delivered through synchronous chat. In their study, 19 individuals with chronic physical disabilities were assigned to a CMC group and compared with a wait-list control group. The participants in the treatment group reported less loneliness at post-test than the control group. These clients maintained this reduction in loneliness in a four-month follow-up.

Barak and Wander-Schwartz (1999) examined the effectiveness of online group therapy. To do so they assigned six college students from Israeli universities to an Internet password-protected synchronous chat-room therapy group and nine to a standard FtF group. Both groups met for seven consecutive weekly sessions. These groups were compared to a control group made up of seven individuals who received no treatment. The results revealed a small but statistically insignificant positive improvement in participants' self-image, social relations and well-being for both the treatment groups. There was a trend in favour of the online group therapy participants. There were generally no changes for individuals in the no-treatment control group. Furthermore, Barak and Wander-Schwartz found several group processes to be similar between the therapy groups, including cohesiveness, personal exposure, expression of feelings, independence, order and organisation. The online group therapy participants reported higher levels of aggression, action orientation and therapist support and control compared to the FtF participants. The theorists concluded that individuals in both the treatment groups demonstrated general satisfaction with their respective group therapies.

The therapeutic relationship

Only a handful of studies have examined the type of relationship or therapeutic alliance that can be formed during online counselling. These few studies have produced mixed results. Hufford *et al.* (1999) compared videoconferencing counselling and FtF therapy for families with epileptic teenagers. The teenagers in the videoconferencing condition reported significantly lower alliance levels than those engaging in FtF therapy. In contrast, Cohen and Kerr (1998) found no significant differences between the CMC and FtF condition regarding individuals' ratings of therapists' expertness, attractiveness and trustworthiness. Cook and Doyle (2002) also found no significant differences between alliances formed in FtF therapy and CMC therapy. In their study those in the CMC condition were either counselled through asynchronous e-mail or synchronous chat.

Making online counselling more effective

Several counsellors and researchers have attempted to identify key points that they believe will improve the effectiveness of online counselling. Some of these are obvious, such as training counsellors and clients in computing and typing skills. Clients might also need to be taught how to communicate effectively in a text-based environment (e.g. learning how to convey emotions through text). Other key issues (described below) are either speculations or theories that have yet to be thoroughly researched.

Suler (2004b) has argued that both clients and therapists should consider the '24-hour rule':

> When people receive a message that stirs them up emotionally, they might apply what I call the 24-Hour Rule. They may compose a reply without sending it (or write nothing), wait 24 hours, then go back to reread the other person's message and their unsent reply. 'Sleeping on it' may help process the situation on a deeper, more insightful level. The next day, from the new temporal perspective, they may interpret the other person's message differently, sometimes less emotionally. The reply they do send off may be very different – hopefully much more rational and mature – than the one they would have sent the day before.
>
> (p. 26)

Setting ground rules and making this transparent to the client is also important. Suler (2004b) points out that counselling is traditionally set within set timeframes (e.g. a weekly one-hour session). With asynchronous communication (e.g. e-mail) clients can send e-mails at any time and as many as they desire. Suler (2004b) states that 'because online therapists run the risk of being overwhelmed with messages from the client, or having the client drift away, they must be careful to create guidelines for an effective, reliable, manageable pacing of messages' (p. 27). Hence, a sensible approach might be to limit the number of e-mails sent and outline clearly when the client should expect to receive a response.

Stofle and Chchele (2004) have also discussed the importance of setting clear guidelines and rules for clients. For example, they suggest that sessional contracts are necessary for online chat therapy. They believe that at the beginning of each chat session the therapist and client need to develop a plan of action for what they will work through in that session and it is the therapist's responsibility to ensure they stick to this contract.

Some researchers have also considered whether a counsellor ought to move from FtF counselling to online counselling. Mallen (2004) points out that early research claimed that 'suddenly shifting an existing f2f [face-to-face] therapeutic relationship to a computer-mediated environment is not ideal for therapeutic outcomes' (p. 73). However, if we consider Yager's

(2001) work (described earlier in this chapter) with anorexia nervosa clients, we see evidence to the contrary. Vacillating between FtF and e-mail worked well for his clients. Perhaps this has to do with combining rather than moving permanently to online counselling. Moreover, in deciding whether one should move from one mode to another the counsellor ought to consider the type of client they are seeing and their presenting problems.

Legal and ethical issues

Professional organisations such as the Australian Psychological Society (APS) and the British Psychological Society (BPS) have made attempts to set out guidelines for online counselling. In addition to these professional groups, independent organisations such as the International Society for Mental Health Online (ISMHO) and the Psychiatric Society for Informatics (PSI) have been set up to work proactively toward passage of legislation as well as considerations of ethical guidelines for online counsellors. PSI was founded in May 1995 and is composed exclusively of psychiatrists, whereas ISMHO was set up in August 1997 and is an interdisciplinary organisation. ISMHO has prepared detailed guidelines for informational mental health and its goal is to guide both the online therapist as well as online clients. Of course, not all the guidelines are yet set in stone and further research is necessary for the development of these guidelines.

One question raised in respect to best online practice is whether a therapist ought to know their client's identity. Being anonymous has certain appeals for online clients. However, some researchers believe that therapists should insist on knowing the identity of their client (e.g. Kraus 2004; Mallen *et al.* 2005). Some of the reasons for this include the client's safety (e.g. to be better equipped to assist the client if they are about to self-harm or harm others), and to avoid a dual relationship (e.g. entering into a counselling relationship with a family member or colleague).

Some theorists have stressed the importance of informed consent from the outset of therapy (e.g. Mallen *et al.* 2005). Such a form should detail an agreement between the client and the therapist in regard to what will be done in the case of an emergency or crisis. In addition, some theorists argue that it should include home address details of the client, their telephone number, physician and emergency contacts (Mallen *et al.* 2005).

Another ethical concern is that of confidentiality (Mallen *et al.* 2005). If counselling sessions are conducted via e-mail, chat or IM, these sessions are recordable and can be saved by both client and therapist. A therapist needs to inform the client that they can only protect their confidentiality to a certain extent. Moreover, they should suggest that clients use a private e-mail account and not e-mail them or engage in therapy at work (where an employer might be entitled to read the transcripts). Mallen *et al.* (2005) warn that 'with a saved transcript, it may be possible for lawyers to use quotes out of context in a trial without needing to question or to have the counseling psychologist present' (p. 783).

A legal concern when it comes to online counselling is who can a therapist conduct therapy with. Does the client need to live in the same state or country as the therapist? Mallen *et al.* (2005) have stated that the 'ability to meet with clients around the world may be enticing, but the legal risks could be extremely costly' (p. 780). Not all laws in every country allow counsellors to practise outside their state or country. Moreover, insurance might not cover a therapist if they practise beyond their state or country.

The future of online counselling

In the future the ethical and legal issues raised here (plus many more) will need to be thoroughly addressed. In addition, further research is needed on the effectiveness of online counselling and how it might be improved. Some researchers have also made a few predictions as to how they perceive the future of online counselling. Holmes and Ainsworth (2004) 'predict that online treatment programs targeting specific problem areas will become even more popular. In many cases the Internet will provide only a portion of treatment, with telephone interviews, printed materials, and face-to-face (f2f) sessions also being included' (p. 260).

Improvements in technology will also shape the future of online counselling. Gross and Anthony (2002) predict that one way forward is *avatar therapy*. An avatar is a computer-generated visible representation of a human or character that represents a 'real' human. While communicating online, instead of seeing a 'real' video image of that person one sees a computer-generated image of the person. The avatar can be dynamic and can replicate the 'real' person's physical movements and emotional expressions. An avatar can allow both the client and therapist some anonymity, while still witnessing important non-verbal cues. Gross and Anthony (2002) argue that there are two possible uses for avatar therapy:

> One is its possible use in conjunction with the current attempts to provide CBT by a computer without the aid of a therapist. . . . The second possibility, which is perhaps less dependent on creating avatars that are quite so naturally looking, might be for group therapy.
>
> (p. 14)

Conclusions

Psychologists need to consider who is best suited for online counselling and the more effective ways of practising this form of therapy. Further research is needed to examine the therapeutic relationships and what gains there are to be made from this type of counselling. It might be that different forms

of online counselling suit different types of clients. Moreover, new technological advancements will provide further options for both therapists and
clients.

13 Concluding thoughts

At the start of this book we introduced the notion of a truth–lies paradox presented by the Internet. Technology that enables truth also, paradoxically, facilitates all kinds of deception. When faced with the choices that life online presents us with, we need to deal with this paradox both in selecting how we ourselves behave, and also how we interpret the actions and intentions of others. For this reason, we have placed trust as pivotal to solving the truth–lies paradox. As discussed earlier, trust is only really critical when there is both uncertainty and potential risk. Online much is uncertain, and this uncertainty carries with it a gamut of risks, ranging from phishing to spam deluges to physical harm.

We know well the technological features of the Internet that enable the truth–lies paradox. While anonymity in its various guises is the most often discussed, geographic distance, asynchronicity and the norms of a particular environment all contribute to the possibility of both truth-telling and lie-making. So, if the technology itself is both an enabler of honesty and deceit, one needs to look beyond explanations rooted in technological determinism in order to fully understand people's behaviour online. Specifically, we would argue that to understand the nature of truth and lies online, one needs to look at the context in which people act alongside the person themselves. We would also argue strongly that truth and lies are not mutually exclusive, and that in much online interaction people are strategically managing their online identity to meet both their own goals and the expectations of the other. While doing this, they are also balancing their actions with the norms for the site or community in which they are active. Take for instance online dating. As we saw earlier in the book, people posting online profiles need to balance truth and lies in such a way as to appear attractive, while also presenting themselves in an accurate way. Thus, we might see self-presentation through omission, or slight exaggeration, but probably not through gross misrepresentation.

As noted above, we have placed trust as central to the truth–lies paradox. For a person presenting themselves online, the affordances of the technology and subsequent possibility for deception pose a unique challenge for establishing trustworthiness, authenticity and legitimacy. This trust can be established in a number of ways, including through the use of specific forms of language and increased self-disclosure, as well as by moving to a richer medium that conveys more cues to identity. In this sense, McLuhan's argument that the 'medium is the message' holds true. The movement through different media seen amongst online daters not only adds new dimensions to the interaction (e.g. sychronicity, voice and visual cues), but also conveys information in itself. So, by giving someone your telephone number not only are you shifting to a more immediate form of communication, but you are also telling the person that you trust them, and that they can trust you. In face-to-face interaction, these different mechanisms for the establishment of trust might be divided into signals and symbols. A signal is something 'given off' during the process of interaction as a byproduct. Meanwhile, a symbol has an assigned meaning like, for instance, a uniform for law enforcement officers. While much of the focus within e-commerce has been on the development of universal symbols (e.g. third party verification services like TRUSTe), when we consider person-to-person interaction, signals may provide a more useful way to think about trust online. Many of the ways in which people assess trust (for instance, in online dating scenarios) could be best characterised as 'signal detection'. That is, people are seeking to distinguish signals of trustworthiness from the noise of interaction. Theoretically, the ability of people to detect this trust signal depends not only on their own abilities, but also on the strength of the signal and the amount of 'noise'. By thinking about trust online in this way, we highlight the importance of viewing not only the source or the target but rather both parties simultaneously.

The critical question facing those who design Internet services is whether or not trust can be designed into systems without losing the benefits of privacy and freedom of expression provided by anonymous and pseudonymous environments. Perhaps first it is important to recognise that in many circumstances trust does not require touch, but it does require time. Studies of computer mediated communication that place strangers in new situations in order to study trust are bound to fail if time is not allowed for 'off-message' activities that build trust. Similarly, online dating profiles that shout 'you can trust me!' are not likely to become a substitute for a prolonged period of interaction. To an extent, the same processes occur with other ways in which we use the Internet; for example, politics, e-commerce and seeking health information online. We have touched upon all these topics in this book. When it comes to e-commerce, for instance, trust is more than a single decision, it is an ongoing process. However, we can shorten the process by designing systems that allow us to use other people's trust experiences as a proxy for our own experiences. The eBay reputation system and reviews of websites provide a history of trust (or lost trust) that can act instead of prolonged interaction. Trust cues – for instance, to competence or integrity – can also be designed into websites. Social systems that provide a sense of a person's historical behaviour (like reputation tracking systems) can also act as a proxy for the building of a trusting relationship. However, it is important to note that trust does not end with a single action (e.g. a purchase, disclosure or contact). Much of the literature about trust online has tended to assume that interactions end, whereas in reality a decision to act based on a trust judgement is often the start of a relationship with multiple trust-critical points.

New developments in Internet-based technology will also pose critical issues for the truth–lies paradox and trust. For instance, location based services in mobile phones, especially peer-to-peer systems, will provide many opportunities for people to be honest or deceitful about their location, as well as requiring them to make fine-grained judgements related to trust in the person or organisation requesting location information. The rise of Web 2.0 services, with their focus on personal disclosure of information, poses critical issues not only about privacy but also about trust in the service provider and the users of the service and information provided by other people. How we present ourselves on these sites can have a larger impact on our lives than first seems immediately obvious. The semantic web and slow addition of meaning to web content will inevitably introduce new questions not only about how much you trust the information provided by users, but also how much you trust the semantic service to accurately convey meaning. As we begin to use automated agents to conduct aspects of our lives for us, much of the fine-grained balancing of truth and lies will need to be integrated into socially aware computer programs, which know when to tell the truth and when to deceive on our behalf. Obviously, not only will we need to trust these same agents to act appropriately, but the agents themselves will need a trust mechanism in order to know who to disclose information to and who to avoid.

As the Internet becomes ever more entangled in our lives, issues of truth, lies and trust will become increasingly important – not only in understanding how people behave online, but also in the design of socially aware systems that act on our behalf. We hope this book has gone some way towards outlining what we believe are likely to be critical questions for the study and use of the Internet in the future.

References

Acquisti, A., & Grossklags, J. (2003). Losses, gains, and hyperbolic discounting: An experimental approach to information security attitudes and behavior. *2nd Annual Workshop on 'Economics and Information Security'*.

Aiken, M., & Waller, B. (2000). Flaming among first-time group support system users. *Information and Management, 37*, 95–100.

Albright, J. M. (2007). How do I love thee and thee and thee: Self-presentation, deception, and multiple relationships online. In M. T. Whitty, A. J. Baker, & J. A. Inman (Eds), *Online matchmaking* (pp. 81–93). Basingstoke: Palgrave Macmillan.

Altman, I. (1973). Reciprocity of interpersonal exchange. *Journal of Theory of Social Behavior, 3* (2), 249–261.

Altman, I. (1975). *The environment and social behavior*. Monterey, CA: Brooks/Cole.

Altman, I. (1977). Privacy regulation: Culturally universal or culturally specific? *Journal of Social Issues, 33* (3), 66–84.

Altman, I., & Taylor, D. (1973). *Social penetration: The development of interpersonal relationships*. New York: Holt, Rinehart and Winston.

Amato, P. R., & Previti, D. (2003). People's reasons for divorcing: Gender, social class, the life course, and adjustment. *Journal of Family Issues, 24* (5), 602–626.

Ando, R., & Sakamoto, A. (2008). The effect of cyber-friends on loneliness and social anxiety: Differences between high and low self-evaluated physical attractiveness groups. *Computers in Human Behavior, 24* (3), 993–1009.

Andrade, E. B., Kaltcheva, V., & Weitz, B. (2002). Self-disclosure on the web: The impact of privacy policy, reward, and company reputation. *Advances in Consumer Research, 29*, 350–353.

Andrejevic, M. (2006). [Monitoring Survey]. Unpublished raw data.

Ang, L., & Lee, B.-C. (2000). Influencing perceptions of trustworthiness in Internet commerce: A rational choice framework. In *Proceedings of Fifth CollECTer Conference on Electronic Commerce* (pp. 1–12), Brisbane.

Antaki, C., Barnes, R., & Leudar, I. (2005). Self-disclosure as a situated interactional practice. *British Journal of Social Psychology, 44*, 181–200.

Anti-Phishing Working Group (2006). *Phishing Activity Trends Report*, July. Retrieved October 26, 2007 from: http://www.antiphishing.org.

Archer, R. L. (1976). Role of personality and the social situation. In G. J. Chelune (Ed.), *Self-disclosure: Origins, patterns and implications of openness in interpersonal relationships* (pp. 28–58). San Francisco: Jossey-Bass.

Argyle, M., & Dean, J. (1965). Eye-contact, distance and affiliation. *Sociometry*, *28*, 289–304.

Arvidsson, A. (2006). 'Quality singles': Internet dating and the work of fantasy. *New Media and Society*, *8* (4), 671–690.

Bad Subjects Production Team (1995). A manifest for bad subjects in cyberspace. Retrieved October 26, 2007 from: http://bad.eserver.org/issues/1995/18/manifesto.html.

Baker, J. (2005). Control alt divorce – how Internet affairs can ruin your marriage. *Sydney Morning Herald*, August 10, 2005. Retrieved August 20, 2005 from: http://www.smh.com.au/news/technology/control-alt-divorce--how-internet-affairs-can-ruin-your-marriage/2005/08/19/1124435144927.html.

Barak, A. (2005). Sexual harassment on the Internet. *Social Science Computer Review*, *23* (1), 77–92.

Barak, A. (2007). Emotional support and suicide prevention through the Internet: A field project report. *Computers in Human Behavior*, *23*, 971–984.

Barak, A., & Dolev-Cohen, M. (2006). Does activity level in online support groups for distressed adolescents determine emotional relief? *Counselling and Psychotherapy Research*, *6*, 186–190.

Barak, A., & Miron, O. (2005). Writing characteristics of suicidal people on the internet. A psychological investigation of emerging social environments. *Suicide and Life-threatening Behaviour*, *35*, 507–524.

Barak, A., & Wander-Schwartz, M. (1999). Empirical evaluation of brief group therapy through an Internet chat room. Retrieved December 27, 2005 from: http://www.brandeis.edu/pubs/jove/HTML/v5/cherapy3.htm.

Bargh, J. A., & McKenna, K. Y. A. (2004). The Internet and social life. *Annual Review of Psychology*, *55*, 573–590.

Bargh, J. A., McKenna, K. Y. A., & Fitzsimons, G. M. (2002). Can you see the real me? Activation and expression of the 'true self' on the internet. *Journal of Social Issues*, *58* (1), 33–48.

BBC News (1999). Cyberstalking: Pursued in cyber space. *BBC News*, 26 June. Retrieved November 16, 2005 from: http://news.bbc.co.uk/1/hi/uk/378373.stm.

BBC News (2005). Man gets nine years for spamming. *BBC News*, 9 April. Retrieved October 5, 2006 from: http://news.bbc.co.uk/1/hi/world/americas/4426949.stm.

BBC News (2006). eBay car buyer robbed at gunpoint. *BBC News*, August. Retrieved October 16, 2006 from: http://news.bbc.co.uk/1/hi/england/5294882.stm.

BBC News (2006). Boy, three, buys car on internet. *BBC News*, September. Retrieved October 10, 2006 from: http://news.bbc.co.uk/1/hi/england/lincolnshire/5379930.stm.

BBC News (2007). Unruly students' facebook search. *BBC News*, July. Retrieved September 19, 2007 from: http://news.bbc.co.uk/1/hi/education/6902333.stm.

Bellafiore, D. R., Colón, Y., & Rosenberg, P. (2004). Online counseling groups. In R. Kraus, J. S. Zack, & G. Stricker (Eds), *Online counselling: A handbook for mental health professionals* (pp. 197–216). San Diego, CA: Elsevier Academic Press.

Ben-Ze'ev, A. (2003). Privacy, emotional closeness, and openness in cyberspace. *Computers in Human Behavior*, *19*, 451–467.

Berger, C. R., & Calabrese, R. J. (1975). Some explorations in initial interaction and beyond: Toward a developmental theory of interpersonal communication. *Human Communication Theory, 1,* 99–112.

Bhattacherjee, A. (2002). Individual trust in online firms: Scale development and initial test. *Journal of Management Information Systems, 19,* 211–241.

Blanchard, A. L., & Henle, C. A. (2008). Correlates of different forms of cyber-loafing: The role of norms and external locus of control. *Computers in Human Behavior, 24* (3), 1067–1084.

Blank, T. O., & Adams-Blodnieks, M. (in press). The who and what of usage of two cancer online communities. *Computers and Human Behavior, 23* (3), 1249–1257.

Bocij, P. (2003). Victims of cyberstalking: An exploratory study of harassment perpetrated via the Internet, 8 (10). Retrieved November 20, 2005 from: http://firstmonday.org/issues/issue8_10/bocij/.

Bocij, P. (2004). *Cyberstalking: Harassment in the internet age and how to protect your family.* Westport, CT: Praeger.

Bok, S. (1989). *Lying: Moral choice in public and private life.* New York: Vintage Books.

Booth-Kewley, S., Edwards, J. E., & Rosenfeld, P. (1992). Impression management, social desirability, and computer administration of attitude questionnaires: Does the computer make a difference? *Journal of Applied Psychology, 77,* 562–566.

Bos, N., Olson, J. S., Gergle, D., Olson, G. M., & Wright, Z. (2002). Rich media helps trust development. In *Proceedings of CHI 2002* (pp. 135–140). New York: ACM Press.

Boyd, J. (2002). In community we trust: Online security communication at eBay. *Journal of Computer Mediated Communication, 7* (3): Retrieved October 15, 2006 from: http://jcmc.indiana.edu/vol7/issue3/boyd.html.

Braithwaite, D. O., Waldron, V. R., & Finn, J. (1999). Communication of social support in computer-mediated groups for people with disabilities. *Health Communication, 11,* 123–151.

Briggs, P., Burford, B., De Angeli, A., & Lynch, P. (2002). Trust in online advice. *Social Science Computer Review, 20* (3), 321–332.

Bruckman, A. (2002). Studying the amateur artist: A perspective on disguising data collected in human subjects research on the Internet. *Ethics and Information Technology, 4* (3), 217–231.

Buller, D. B., & Burgoon, J. K. (1996). Interpersonal deception theory. *Communication Theory, 6,* 203–242.

Burgoon, J. K., Parrott, R., LePoire, B. A., Kelley, D. L., Walther, J. B., & Perry, D. (1989). Maintaining and restoring privacy through communication in different types of relationship. *Journal of Social and Personal Relationships, 6,* 131–158.

Buss, D. M. (2000). Desires in human mating. *Annals New York Academy of Sciences, 907,* 39–49.

Caspi, A., & Gorsky, P. (2006). Online deception: Prevalence, motivation, and emotion. *CyberPsychology and Behavior, 9,* 54–59.

Chang, R. (2005). Online counseling: Prioritizing, psychoeducation, self-help, and mutual help for counseling psychology research and practice. *The Counseling Psychologist, 33* (6), 1–10.

Cheating wife stories–cheating husband stories. Retrieved October 20, 2005 from: http://www.chatcheaters.com/cheating-stories/cheating-stories.html.

Chellappa, R. K., & Sin, R. G. (2005). Personalisation versus privacy: An empirical examination of the online consumer's dilemma. *Information Technology and Management, 6*, 181–202.

Chesney, T. (2005). Online self disclosure in diaries and its implications for knowledge managers. In *UK Academy for Information Systems Conference Proceedings*, 22–24 March, Northumbria University, UK.

Cohen, G. E., & Kerr, B. A. (1998). Computer-mediated counseling: An empirical study of a new mental health treatment. *Computers in Human Services, 15* (4), 13–26.

Cook, J. E., & Doyle, C. (2002). Working alliance in online therapy as compared to face-to-face therapy: Preliminary results. *CyberPsychology and Behavior, 5* (2), 95–105.

Cooper, A. (2002). *Sex & the Internet: A guidebook for clinicians.* New York: Brunner-Routledge.

Cooper, A., Delmonico, D. L., & Burg, R. (2000). Cybersex users, abusers, and compulsives: New findings and implications. *Sexual Addiction and Compulsivity, 7*, 5–29.

Cooper, A., Putnam, D. E., Planchon, L. A., & Boies, S. C. (1999). Online sexual compulsivity: Getting tangled in the net. *Sexual Addiction and Compulsivity, 6*, 79–104.

Cornwell, B., & Lundgren, D. C. (2001). Love on the Internet: Involvement and misrepresentation in romantic relationships in cyberspace vs. realspace. *Computers in Human Behavior, 17*, 197–211.

Corritore, C. L., Kracher, B., & Wiedenbeck, S. (2001). Trust in the online environment. In M. J. Smith, G. Salvendy, D. Harris, & R. J. Koubek (Eds), *Usability evaluation and interface design: Cognitive engineering, intelligent agents and virtual reality* (pp. 1548–1552). Mahwah, NJ: Lawrence Erlbaum Associates, Inc.

Cupach, W. R., & Spitzberg, B. H. (1998). Obsessive relational intrusion and stalking. In B. H. Spitzberg & W. R. Cupach (Eds), *The dark side of close relationships* (pp. 233–263). Mahwah, NJ: Lawrence Erlbaum Associates, Inc.

Cupach, W. R., Spitzberg, B. H., & Carson, C. L. (2000). Toward a theory of stalking and obsessive relational intrusion. In K. Dindia & S. Duck (Eds), *Communication and personal relationships* (pp. 131–146). New York: Wiley.

Cutrona, C. E., & Suhr, J. A. (1992). Controllability of stressful events and satisfaction with spouse support behaviors. *Communication Research, 19*, 154–174.

Daft, R., & Lengel, R. (1986). Organizational information requirements, media richness and structural design. *Management Science, 32* (5), 554–571.

Danet, B. (1998). Text as mask: Gender, play and performance on the internet. In S. G. Jones (Ed.), *Cybersociety 2.0: Revisiting computer-mediated communication and community* (pp. 129–158). Thousand Oaks, CA: Sage.

Dating Sites Reviews.com (n.d.). Retrieved April 13, 2006 from: http://www.datingsitesreviews.com/staticpages/index.php?page=2010000100-FriendFinder.

Davis, R. A. (2001). Cyberslacking: Internet abuse in the workplace. Retrieved June 1, 2003 from: http://www.internetaddiction.ca/cyberslacking.htm.

Davis, R. A., Flett, G. L., & Besser, A. (2002). Validation of a new scale for measuring problematic internet use: Implications for pre-employment screening. *CyberPsychology and Behavior, 5* (4), 331–345.

Day, S. X., & Schneider, P. L. (2002). Psychotherapy using distance technology: A comparison of face-to-face, video, and audio treatment. *Journal of Counseling Psychology, 49* (4), 499–503.

DeBurgher, J. (1972). Sex in troubled marriages. *Sexual Behavior, 2,* 23–26.

DeCew, J. (1997). *In Pursuit of Privacy: Law, Ethics, and the Rise of Technology.* Ithaca: Cornell University Press.

Deirmenjian, J. M. (1999). Stalking in cyberspace. *Journal of the American Academy of Psychiatry and the Law, 27* (3), 407–413.

Delmonico, D. L., Griffin, E. J., & Carnes, P. J. (2002). Treating online compulsive sexual behavior: When cybersex becomes the drug of choice. In A. Cooper (Ed.), *Sex and the internet: A guidebook for clinicians* (pp. 147–167). New York: Taylor & Francis.

DePaulo, B. M., & Kashy, D. A. (1998). Everyday lies in close and casual relationships. *Journal of Personality and Social Psychology, 74,* 63–79.

DePaulo, B. M., Kashy, D. A., Kirkendol, S. E., Wyer, M. M., & Epstein, J. A. (1996). Lying in everyday life. *Journal of Personality and Social Psychology, 70,* 979–995.

DePaulo, B. M., Wetzel, C., Sternglanz, W. R., & Wilson, M. J. W. (2003). Verbal and nonverbal dynamics of privacy, secrecy, and deceit. *Journal of Social Issues, 59* (2), 391–410.

Derlega, V. L., & Chaikin, A. L. (1977). Privacy and self-disclosure in social relationships. *Journal of Social Issues, 33,* 102–115.

Des Jarlais, D. C., Paone, D., Milliken, J., Turner, C. F., Miller, H., Gribble, J., Shi, Q., Hagan, H., & Friedman, S. (1999). Audio-computer interviewing to measure risk behaviour for HIV among injecting drug users: A quasi-randomised trial. *The Lancet, 353* (9165), 1657–1661.

DeSteno, D., Bartlett, M. Y., Braverman, J., & Salovey, P. (2002). Sex differences in jealousy: Evolutionary mechanism or artifact of measurement? *Journal of Personality and Social Psychology, 83* (5), 1103–1116.

DeSteno, D., & Salovey, P. (1996). Evolutionary origins of sex differences in jealousy? Questioning the 'fitness' of the model. *Psychological Science, 7,* 367–371.

Deutsch, M. (1962). Cooperation and trust: Some theoretical notes. *Nebraska Symposium on Motivation, 10,* 275–318.

Dhamija, R., Tygar, J. D., & Hearst, M. (2006). Why phishing works. In *Proceedings of the SIGCHI Conference on Human Factors in Computing Systems.* New York: ACM Press.

Donath, J. S. (1998). Identity and deception in the virtual community. In M. A. Smith & P. Kollock (Eds), *Communities in cyberspace* (pp. 29–59). New York: Routledge.

Duck, S. W. (1991). *Understanding relationships.* New York: Guilford Press.

eBay (n.d.). Community. Retrieved October 17, 2006, from: http://pages.ebay.co.uk/help/community/values.html.

Egger, F. N. (2000).Trust me, I'm an online vendor: Towards a model of trust for e-commerce system design. In *Proceedings of the Conference on Human Factors in Computing Systems* (pp. 101–102). New York: ACM Press.

Elron Software, I. (2001). *The year 2001 corporate web and email usage study.* Retrieved November 12, 2003 from: www.elronsw.com/pdf/NFOReport.pdf.

Epstein, J. F., Barker, P. R., & Kroutil, L. A. (2001). Mode effects in self-reported mental health data. *Public Opinion Quarterly, 65,* 529–550.

Erikson, E. H. (1963). *Childhood and society* (2nd ed.). New York: Norton.

Espy software online. (n.d.). Retrieved March 29, 2006, from http://www.e-spy-software.com/.

Ess, C. (2007). Internet research ethics. In A. Joinson, K. McKenna, T. Postmes, & U.-D., Reips (Eds), *The Oxford handbook of internet psychology* (pp. 487–502). Oxford: Oxford University Press.

Exline, R. V., Gray, D., & Winter, L. C. (1965). Affective relations and mutual glances in dyads. In S. S. Tomkins & C. E. Izard (Eds), *Affect, cognition and personality*. New York: Springer.

Eysenbach, G., Powell, J., Englesakis, M., Rizo, C., & Stern, A. (2004). Health related virtual communities and electronic support groups: systematic review of the effects of online peer to peer interactions. *British Medical Journal*, 15 May 2004. Retrieved December 27, 2005 from: 328:1166, doi:10.1136/bmj.328.7449.1166.

Feldman, M. D. (2000). Munchausen by internet: Detecting factitious illness and crisis on the internet. *Southern Medical Journal*, *93*, 669–672.

Fenichel, M. A. (2004). Online behaviour, communication, and experience. In R. Kraus, J. S. Zack, & G. Stricker (Eds), *Online counselling: A handbook for mental health professionals* (pp. 51–68). San Diego, CA: Elsevier Academic Press.

Ferriter, M. (1993). Computer aided interviewing and the psychiatric social history. *Social Work and Social Sciences Review*, *4*, 255–263.

Finextra (2006). UK phishing fraud losses double. 7 March. Retrieved April 14, 2007 from: http://www.finextra.com/fullstory.asp?id=15013.

Finn, J. (1999). An exploration of helping processes in an online self-help group focusing on issues of disability. *Health and Social Work*, *24*, 220–231.

Fischer, C. S. (1992). *America calling: A social history of the telephone to 1940*. Berkley, CA: University of California Press.

Fisher, V. (2002). Is it OK to monitor employees? *ZDNet Australia*, 10 July 2002. Retrieved September 29, 2002 from: http://news.zdnet.co.uk/story/0,,t300-s2118847,00.html.

Fitness, J. (2001). Betrayal, rejection, revenge and forgiveness: An interpersonal script approach. In M. Leary (Ed.), *Interpersonal rejection* (pp. 73–103). New York: Oxford University Press.

Fogg, B. J., Marshall, J., Laraki, O., Osipovich, A., Varma, C., Fang, N., Paul, J., Rangnekar, A., Shon, J., Swani, P., & Treinen, M. (2001). What makes web sites credible? A report on a large quantitative study. In *Proceedings of the Conference on Human Factors in Computing Systems* (pp. 61–68). New York: ACM Press.

Former Girlfriends. Retrieved November 20, 2005 from: http://www.formergirlfriends.com/index.php.

Fox, S., & Schwartz, D. (2002). Social desirability and controllability in computerized and paper-and-pencil personality questionnaires. *Computers in Human Behavior*, *18*, 389–410.

Franzoi, S. L., & Davis, M. H. (1985). Adolescent self-disclosure and loneliness: Private self-consciousness and parental influences. *Journal of Personality and Social Psychology*, *48*, 768–780.

Frick, A., Bächtiger, M. T., & Reips, U.-D. (2001). Financial incentives, personal information and drop-out in online studies. In U.-D. Reips & M. Bosnjak (Eds), *Dimensions of internet science* (pp. 209–219). Lengerich: Pabst.

Galegher, J., Sproull, L., & Kiesler, S. (1998). Legitimacy, authority, and community in electronic support groups. *Written Communication*, *15*, 493–530.

Gavison, R. (1980). Privacy and the limits of law. *Yale Law Journal*, *89*, 421–471.

Gefen, D. (2002). Reflections on the dimensions of trust and trustworthiness among online consumers. *ACM SIGMIS Database*, *33* (3), 38–53.

Glass, G., & Wright, T. (1985). Sex differences in type of extramarital involvement and marital dissatisfaction. *Sex Roles*, *12*, 1101–1120.

Goldring, J., Adams, M., Graycar, R., & Ross, I. (2001). *Surveillance: An interim report*. Sydney: Law Reform Commission Publications.

Gonyea, J. L. J. (2004). Internet sexuality: Clinical implications for couples. *American Journal of Family Therapy*, *32* (5), 375–390.

Green, M. (2007). Trust and social interaction on the Internet. In A. N. Joinson, K. Y. A. McKenna, T. Postmes, & U.-R. Reips, *Oxford handbook of internet psychology* (pp. 43–51). Oxford: Oxford University Press.

Greenfield, D. N., & Davis, R. A. (2002). Lost in cyberspace: The web @ work. *CyberPsychology and Behavior*, *5* (4), 347–353.

Greengard, S. (2000). The high cost of cyberslacking. *Workforce*, *79*, 22–24.

Greist, J. H., Klein, M. H., & VanCura, L. J. (1973). A computer interview by psychiatric patient target symptoms. *Archives of General Psychiatry*, *29*, 247–253.

Griffiths, M. (1999). Internet addiction: Fact or fiction. *Psychologist*, *12*, 246–250.

Griffiths, M. (2000a). Excessive Internet use: Implications for sexual behaviour. *CyberPsychology and Behavior*, *3* (4), 537–552.

Griffiths, M. (2000b). Internet addiction – time to be taken seriously? *Addiction Research*, *8*, 413–418.

Griffiths, M. D. (2001). Sex on the internet: Observations and implications for sex addiction. *Journal of Sex Research*, *38*, 333–342.

Griffiths, M. (2003). Internet abuse in the workplace: Issues and concerns for employers and employment counselors. *Journal of Employment Counseling*, *40* (2), 87–96.

Griffiths, M. D. (2004). Hi-tech gambling scams. *The Criminal Lawyer*, *140*, 4–5.

Grohol, J. M. (1998). Response to the HomeNet study: *PsychCentral*. Retrieved October 27, 2004 from: http://psychcentral.com/homenet.htm.

Grohol, J. M. (2004). Online counseling: A historical perspective. In R. Kraus, J. S. Zack, & G. Stricker (Eds), *Online counselling: A handbook for mental health professionals* (pp. 51–68). San Diego, CA: Elsevier Academic Press.

Gross, E. F., Juvonen, J., & Gable, S. L. (2002). Internet use and well-being in adolescence. *Journal of Social Issues*, *58* (1), 75–90.

Gross, S., & Anthony, K. (2002). Virtual counsellors – whatever next? *Counselling Journal*, *13* (2), 14–15.

Hamburger, Y. A., & Ben-Artzi, E. (2003). Loneliness and Internet use. *Computers in Human Behavior*, *19*, 71–80.

Hampton, K., & Wellman, B. (2003). Neighboring in netville: How the Internet supports community and social capital in a wired suburb. *City and Community*, *2* (4), 277–311.

Hancock, J. (2007). Digital deception. In A. N. Joinson, K. McKenna, T. Postmes, & U.-D. Reips (Eds), *Oxford handbook of internet psychology* (pp. 289–301). Oxford: Oxford University Press.

Hancock, J. T., Curry, L., Goorha, S., & Woodworth, M. (2005). An automated linguistic analysis of deceptive and truthful computer-mediated communication. *Proceedings of the Hawaii International Conference on System Sciences.*

Hancock, J. T., Thom-Santelli, J., & Ritchie, T. (2004). Deception and design: The impact of communication technologies on lying behavior (pp. 130–136). *Proceedings of the Conference on Computer Human Interaction.* New York: ACM Press.

Hancock, J. T., Toma, C., & Ellison, N. (2007). The truth about lying in online dating profiles (pp. 449–452). *Proceedings of the ACM Conference on Human Factors in Computing Systems.*

Handy, C. (1995). Trust and the virtual organization. *Harvard Business Review, 73* (3), 40–50.

Hansen, G. (1987). Extradyadic relations during courtship. *Journal of Sex Research, 23* (3), 382–390.

Harper, V. B., & Harper, E. J. (2006). Understanding student self-disclosure typology through blogging. *The Qualitative Report, 11* (2), 251–261.

Harris and Associates (2002). First major post-9-11 privacy survey finds consumers demanding companies do more to protect privacy; public wants company privacy policies to be independently verified. Retrieved June 20, 2005 from: http://www.harrisinteractive.com/news/allnewsbydate.asp?NewsID=429.

Harris, C. R. (2004). The evolution of jealousy: Did men and women, facing different selective pressures, evolve different 'brands' of jealousy? Recent evidence suggests not. *American Scientist, 92,* 62–71.

Harris, C. R., & Christenfeld, N. (1996). Gender, jealousy, and reason. *Psychological Science, 7* (6), 364–245.

Harris Interactive (2004). Therapy in America 2004. Retrieved December 27, 2005 from: http://www.harrisinteractive.com/industries/pubs/Pacificare_Behavioral_Health_Psychology_Today.pdf.

Herring, S. C. (1993). Gender and democracy in computer-mediated communication. *Electronic Journal of Communication (online) 3* (2). Retrieved October 26, 2005 from: http://www.cios.org/EJCPUBLIC$$736732983732$$/003/2/00328. HTML.

Hertlein, K. M., & Piercy, F. P. (2006). Internet infidelity: A critical review of the literature. *The Family Journal, 14,* 266–371.

Higgins, E. T. (1987). Self-discrepancy theory. *Psychological Review, 94* (3), 1120–1134.

Hiltz, S. R., Johnson, M., & Turoff, M. (1986). Experiments in group decision making: Communication process and outcome in face-to-face versus computerized conferences. *Human Communication Research, 13,* 225–252.

Hiltz, S. R., & Turoff, M. (1978). *The network nation: Human communication via computers.* Reading, MA: Addison-Wesley.

Hoffman, D. L., Novak, T. P., & Peralta, M. (1999). Building consumer trust online. *Communications of the ACM, 42,* 80–85.

Holmes, L., & Ainsworth, M. (2004). The future of online counseling. In R. Kraus, J. S. Zack, & G. Stricker (Eds), *Online counselling: A handbook for mental health professionals* (pp. 257–269). San Diego, CA: Elsevier Academic Press.

Holmes, J. G., & Rempel, J. K. (1989). Trust in close relationships. In C. Hendrick (Ed.), *Close relationships: Review of personality and social psychology* (Vol. 10, pp. 187–220). Newbury Park, CA: Sage.

Hopps, S. L., Pepin, M., & Boisvert, J. (2003). The effectiveness of cognitive-behavioral group therapy for loneliness via inter relay chat among people with physical disabilities. *Psychotherapy: Theory, Research, Practice, Training, 40* (1/2), 136–147.

Hsiung, R. C. (2000). The best of both worlds: An online self-help group hosted by a mental health professional. *CyberPsychology and Behavior, 3* (6), 935–950.

Hudson, J. M., & Bruckman, A. (2004). 'Go away': Participant objections to being studied and the ethics of chatroom research. *The Information Society, 20,* 127–139.

Hufford, B. J., Glueckauf, R. L., & Webb, P. M. (1999). Home-based, interactive videoconferencing for adolescents with epilepsy and their families. *Rehabilitation Psychology, 44* (2), 176–193.

Ingham, R. (1978). Privacy and psychology. In J. B. Young (Ed.), *Privacy* (pp. 35–59). Chichester: Wiley.

Jarvenpaa, S. L., Knoll, K., & Leidner, D. E. (1998). Is anybody out there? Antecedents of trust in global virtual teams. *Journal of Management Information Systems, 14,* 29–64.

Jarvenpaa, S. L., Tractinsky, J., & Saarinen, L. (1999). Consumer trust in an Internet store: A cross-cultural validation. *Journal of Computer Mediated Communication [on-line serial], 5* (2).

Joinson, A. N. (1999). Anonymity, disinhibition and social desirability on the Internet. *Behaviour Research Methods, Instruments and Computers, 31,* 433–438.

Joinson, A. N. (2001). Self-disclosure in computer-mediated communication: The role of self-awareness and visual anonymity. *European Journal of Social Psychology, 31,* 177–192.

Joinson, A. N. (2003). *Understanding the psychology of internet behaviour: Virtual worlds, real lives.* Basingstoke: Palgrave Macmillan.

Joinson, A. N. (2004). Self-esteem, interpersonal risk and preference for e-mail to face-to-face communication. *CyberPsychology and Behaviour, 7,* 472–478.

Joinson, A. N., & Dietz-Uhler, B. (2002). Explanations for the perpetration of and reactions to deception in a virtual community. *Social Science Computer Review, 20* (3), 275–289.

Joinson, A. N, & Paine, C. B. (2007). Self-disclosure, privacy and the Internet. In A. N. Joinson, K. McKenna, T. Postmes, & U.-D. Reips (Eds), *Oxford handbook of internet psychology* (pp. 237–252). Oxford: Oxford University Press.

Joinson, A. N., Paine, C. B., Buchanan, T., & Reips, U.-R. (in press). Measuring self-disclosure online: Blurring and non-responsive to sensitive items in web-based surveys. *Computers and Human Behavior.*

Joinson, A. N., Woodley, A., & Reips, U.-R. (2007). Personalization, authentication and self-disclosure in self-administered Internet surveys. *Computers in Human Behavior, 23,* 275–285.

Jourard, S. M. (1971). *Self-disclosure: An experimental analysis of the transparent self.* New York: Krieger.

Jourard, S. M., & Lasakow, P. (1958). Some factors in self-disclosure. *Journal of Abnormal and Social Psychology, 56* (1), 91–98.

Jupiter Research (2002). Seventy percent of US consumers worry about online privacy, but few take protective action. Retrieved November 20, 2005 from: http://www.jmm.com/xp/jmm/press/2002/pr_060302.xml.

Kamir, O. (1995). Stalking: History, culture & law. SJD dissertation. University of Michigan Law School, Ann Arbor.

Katz, J. E., & Aspden, P. (1997). A nation of strangers. *Communications of the ACM, 40* (12), 81–86.

Kawamoto, D. (2006). Spammers face jail. *CNET News.com*, 4 October. Retrieved October 5, 2006 from: http://news.zdnet.co.uk/internet/security/0,39020375, 39283813,00.htm.

Kerstein, P. (2005). How can we stop phishing and pharming scams? *CSO*, 19 July. Retrieved April 14, 2007 from: http://www.csoonline.com/talkback/071905.html.

Kidwell Jr., R. E., & Bennett, N. (1994). Employee reactions to electronic control systems. *Group and Organization Management, 19* (2), 203–219.

Kiesler, S. J., Siegel, J., & McGuire, T. W. (1984). Social psychological aspects of computer-mediated communication. *American Psychologist, 39*, 1123–1134.

Kitzinger, C., & Powell, D. (1995). Engendering infidelity: Essentialist and social constructionist readings of a story completion task. *Feminism and Psychology, 5* (3), 345–372.

Kraus, R. (2004). Ethical and legal considerations for providers of mental health services online. In R. Kraus, J. S. Zack, & G. Stricker (Eds), *Online counselling: A handbook for mental health professionals* (pp. 51–68). San Diego, CA: Elsevier Academic Press.

Kraus, R., Zack, J., & Stricker, G. (2004). Erratum. In R. Kraus, J. S. Zack, & G. Stricker (Eds), *Online counselling: A handbook for mental health professionals*. San Diego, CA: Elsevier Academic Press.

Kraut, R., Kiesler, S., Boneva, B., Cummings, J. N., Helgeson, V., & Crawford, A. M. (2002). Internet paradox revisited. *Journal of Social Issues, 58*, 49–74.

Kraut, R., Patterson, M., Lundmark, V., Kiesler, S., Mukopadhyay, T., & Scherlies, W. (1998). Internet paradox: A social technology that reduces social involvement and psychological well-being? *American Psychologist, 53*, 1017–1031.

Lamb, M. (1998). Cybersex: Research notes on the characteristics of the visitors to online chat rooms. *Deviant Behavior, 19*, 121–135.

Lange, A., van de Ven, J. P., Schrieken, B., & Emmelkamp, P. M. G. (2001). Interapy, treatment of posttraumatic stress through the Internet: A controlled trial. *Journal of Behavioral Therapy and Experimental Psychiatry, 32* (2), 73–90.

LaPadula, P. (2006). Online hookup sites see thefts, assaults. *The New York Blade*, 8 June. Retrieved June 25, 2006 from: http://www.newyorkblade.com/thelatest/ thelatest.cfm?blog_id=7373.

LaRose, R., Eastin, M., & Gregg, J. (2001). Reformulating the internet paradox: Social cognitive explanations of internet use and depression. *Journal of Online Behavior, 1* (2). Retrieved October 27, 2004 from: http://www.behavior.net/JOB/ v1n2/paradox.html.

Lau, J. T. F., Tsui, H. Y., & Wang, Q. S. (2003). Effects of two telephone survey methods on the level of reported risk behaviours. *Sexually Transmitted Infections, 79*, 325–331.

Laurenceau, J. P., Barrett, L. F., & Pietromonaco, P. R. (1998). Intimacy as an interpersonal process: The importance of self-disclosure, partner disclosure, and perceived partner responsiveness in interpersonal exchanges. *Journal of Personality and Social Psychology, 74*, 1238–1251.

Lawson, H. M., & Leck, K. (2006). Dynamics of internet dating. *Social Science Computer Review, 24* (2), 189–208.

Lea, M., O'Shea, T., Fung, P., & Spears, R. (1992). 'Flaming' in computer-mediated communication. Observations, explanations, implications. In M. Lea (Ed.),

Contexts of computer-mediated communication (pp. 89–112). New York: Harvester Wheatsheaf.

Lessler, J. T., Caspar, R. A., Penne, M. A., & Barker, P. R. (2000). Developing computer assisted interviewing (CAI) for the National Household Survey on Drug Abuse. *Journal of Drug Issues, 30*, 19–34.

Lewis, D., & Weigert, A. (1985). Trust as a social reality. *Social Forces, 63* (4), 967–985.

Leyden, J. (2004). US phishing losses hit $500m. *The Register.* 29 September. Retrieved October 26, 2007 from: http://www.theregister.co.uk/2004/09/29/phishing_survey/.

Lindgaard, G., Fernandes, G., Dudek, C., & Brown, J. (2006). Attention web designers: You have 50 milliseconds to make a good first impression! *Behaviour and Information Technology, 25*, 115–126.

Lloyd-Goldstein, R. (1998). De Clérambault on-line: A survey or erotomania and stalking from the old world to the World Wide Web. In J. R. Meloy (Ed.), *The psychology of stalking* (pp. 193–212). San Diego, CA: Academic Press.

Lyon, D. (2003). *Surveillance after September 11.* Malden, MA: Blackwell.

Maheu, M., & Subotnik, R. (2001). *Infidelity on the internet: Virtual relationships and real betrayal.* Naperville: Sourcebooks.

Malhotra, N. K., Kim, S. S., & Agarwal, J. (2004). Internet users' information privacy concerns (IUIPC): The construct, the scale and a causal model. *Information Systems Research, 15*, 336–355.

Mallen, M. J. (2004). Online counseling research. In R. Kraus, J. S. Zack, & G. Stricker (Eds), *Online counselling: A handbook for mental health professionals* (pp. 70–89). San Diego, California: Elsevier Academic Press.

Mallen, M. J., & Vogel, D. L. (2005). Online counseling: A need for discovery. *The Counseling Psychologist, 33* (6), 910–921.

Mallen, M. J., Vogel, D. L., & Rochlen, A. B. (2005). The practical aspects of online counseling: Ethics, training, technology, and competency. *The Counseling Psychologist, 33* (6), 776–818.

Mallen, M. J., Vogel, D. L., Rochlen, A. B., & Day, S. X. (2005). Online counseling: Reviewing the literature from a counseling psychology framework. *The Counseling Psychologist, 33* (6), 819–871.

Manhal-Baugus, M. (2001). E-therapy: Practical, ethical, and legal issues. *Cyber-Psychology and Behavior, 4* (5), 551–563.

Mann, C., & Stewart, F. (2000). *Internet communication and qualitative research: A handbook for researching online.* London: Sage.

Margulis, S. T. (2003). On the status and contribution of Westin's and Altman's theories of privacy. *Journal of Social Issues, 59*, 411–429.

Matheson, K., & Zanna, M. P. (1988). The impact of computer-mediated communication on self-awareness. *Computers in Human Behaviour, 4*, 221–233.

Mayer, R. C., Davis, J. H., & Schoorman, F. D. (1995). An integrative model of organizational trust. *Academy of Management Review, 20* (3), 709–734.

McGrath, M. G., & Casey, E. (2002). Forensic psychiatry and the internet: Practical perspectives on sexual predators and obsessional harassers in cyberspace. *Journal of the American Academy of Psychiatry and the Law, 20*, 81–94.

McKenna, K. Y. A., & Bargh, J. (1998). Coming out in the age of the Internet: Identity demarginalization through virtual group participation. *Journal of Personality and Social Psychology, 75*, 681–694.

McKenna, K. Y. A., Green, A. S., & Gleason, M. E. J. (2002). Relationship formation on the Internet: What's the big attraction? *Journal of Social Issues, 58* (1), 9–31.

McKnight, D. H., Cummings, L. L., & Chervany, N. L. (1998). Initial trust formation in new organizational relationships. *Academy of Management Review, 23* (3), 473–490.

McLaughlin, M., Osborne, K., & Smith, C. (1995). Standards of conduct on Usenet. In S. Jones (Ed.), *Cybersociety* (pp. 90–111). Thousand Oaks, CA: Sage.

McNealy, S. (1999). Reported in *Wired*, 26 January. Retrieved January 19, 2006 from: http://www.wired.com/news/politics/0,1283,17538,00.html.

Meet2cheat. (n.d.). Retrieved October 31, 2005 from: http://www.meet2cheat.com.au/company/index.htm.

Mehrabian, A., & Ferris, S. R. (1967). Inference of attitudes from nonverbal communication in two channels. *Journal of Consulting Psychology, 31*, 248–252.

Meloy, J. R. (1998). The psychology of stalking. In J. R. Meloy (Ed.), *The psychology of stalking: Clinical and forensic perspectives* (pp. 1–23). San Diego, CA: Academic Press.

Metzger, M. J. (2004). Privacy, trust and disclosure: Exploring barriers to electronic commerce. Accessed 20 June, 2005 from: http://jcmc.indiana.edu/vol9/issue4/metzger.html.

Mileham, B. L. A. (2007). Online infidelity in Internet chat rooms: An ethnographic exploration. *Computers in Human Behavior, 23* (1), 11–21.

Miller, H., & Arnold, J. (2001). Breaking away from grounded identity? Women academics on the web. *CyberPsychology and Behavior, 4* (1), 95–108.

Moon, Y. (1998). Impression management in computer-based interviews: The effects of unput modality, output modality, and distance. *Public Opinion Quarterly, 62*, 610–622.

Moon, Y. (2000). Intimate exchanges: Using computers to elicit self-disclosure from consumers. *Journal of Consumer Research, 27*, 323–339.

Morahan-Martin, J. (1999). The relationship between loneliness and Internet use and abuse. *Cyberpsychology and Behavior, 2*, 431–439.

Morahan-Martin, J., & Schumacher, P. (2003). Loneliness and social uses of the Internet. *Computers in Human Behavior, 19*, 659–671.

News.com.au. (2006). Online baby goods unsafe, says research. Retrieved October 16, 2006 from: http://www.news.com.au/story/0,23599,20594742-1702,00.html.

NHMRC (1999). *National statement on ethical conduct in research involving humans.* Retrieved September 25, 2002 from: http://www.health.gov.au/nhmrc/publications/humans/part17.htm.

Nickel, J., & Schaumburg, H. (2004). Electronic privacy, trust and self-disclosure in e-recruitment. Late breaking results paper presented at CHI 2004, 24–29 April, Vienna, Austria.

Nie, N. H. (2001). Sociability, interpersonal relations, and the Internet: Reconciling conflicting findings. *American Behavioral Scientist, 45* (3), 420–435.

Niederhoffer, K. G., & Pennebaker, J. W. (2001). *Linguistic synchrony in social interaction.* Manuscript submitted for publication.

Nielsen, J., Molich, R., Snyder, C., & Farrell, S. (2000). E-commerce user experience: Trust. Nielsen NormanGroup, Fremont, CA. Retrieved November 25, 2007 from: http://www.nngroup.com/reports/ecommerce/.

Nietzsche, F. (2003). *Beyond good and evil*, trans. R. J. Hollingdale. Harmonds-worth: Penguin. (Original work published 1973.)

NormanGroup, Fremont, CA. Retrieved March 6, 2001 from: http://www.nngroup.com/reports/ecommerce/.

Nosek, B. A., Banaji, M. R., & Greenwald, A. G. (2002). E-research: Ethics, security, design, and control in psychological research on the internet. *Journal of Social Issues, 58* (1), 161–176.

Out my ex.com. Retrieved November 20, 2005 from: http://www.outmyex.com/.

Paine, C. B., Joinson, A. N., Buchanan, T., & Reips, U.-D. (2006). Privacy and self-disclosure online. In *Extended Abstracts of the Conference on Human Factors in Computing Systems* (pp. 1187–1192). Montréal, Canada, April.

Parent, W. (1983). *Privacy, morality and the law. Philosophy and Public Affairs, 12,* 269–288.

Parker, T. S., & Wampler, K. S. (2003). How bad is it? Perceptions of the relationship impact of different types of internet sexual activities. *Contemporary Family Therapy, 25* (4), 415–429.

Parks, M. R., & Floyd, K. (1996). Making friends in cyberspace. *Journal of Communication, 46,* 80–97.

Parks, M. R., & Roberts, L. D. (1998). 'Making MOOsic': The development of personal relationships online and a comparison to their off-line counterparts. *Journal of Social and Personal Relationships, 15,* 517–537.

Pasha, S. (2005). Online dating feeling less attractive. *CNN/Money,* 18 August. Retrieved April 13, 2006 from: http://money.cnn.com/2005/08/18/technology/online_dating/index.htm.

Paul, L., & Galloway, J. (1994). Sexual jealousy: Gender differences in response to partner and rival. *Aggressive Behavior, 20,* 203–211.

Paulhus, D. L. (1984). Two-component models of socially desirable responding. *Journal of Personality and Social Psychology, 46,* 598–609.

Pennebaker, J. W. (1997). Writing about emotional experiences as a therapeutic process. *Psychological Science, 8* (3), 162–166.

Pennebaker, J. W., Kiecolt-Glaser, J. K., & Glaser, R. (1988). Disclosure of traumas and immune function: Health implications for psychotherapy. *Journal of Consulting and Clinical Psychology, 56,* 239–245.

Perkins, P. (2006). Midtowner among film industry targets. Retrieved October 16, 2006 from: http://www.commercialappeal.com/mca/local/article/0,2845,MCA_25340_4997769,00.html.

Pew Internet and American Life Project (2001). Fox, S., Rainie, L. Horrigan, J. Lenhart, A., Spooner, T., & Carter, C. *Trust and privacy online: Why Americans want to rewrite the rules.* Available at http://www.pewinternet.org.

Pew Internet and American Life Project (2005). Health information online. Retrieved October 26, 2006 from: http://www.pewinternet.org/pdfs/PIP_Health-topics_May05.pdf.

Pew Internet and American Life Project (2006). Online Health Search 2006. Retrieved October 16, 2007 from: http://www.pewinternet.org.

Philanderers.com (n.d.). Retrieved October 31, 2005 from: http://www.philanderers.com/.

Powell, W. (2003). Spam wars – an increasing number of computer users are trying to rid the world of spam. *Training and Development,* April. Retrieved October 5, 2006 from: http://findarticles.com/p/articles/mi_m0MNT/is_4_57/ai_99932978.

Preece, J. J., & Ghozati, K. (2001). Experiencing empathy online. In R. E. Rice & J. E. Katz (Eds), *The internet and health communication* (pp. 237–260). Thousand Oaks, CA: Sage.

Putnam, R. D. (1996). The strange disappearance of civic life in America. *American Prospect*, *24*, 34–46.

Putnam, R. D. (2001). *Bowling alone: The collapse and revival of American community*. New York: Simon & Schuster.

RateMyProfessor. (n.d.). Retrieved March 29, 2006 from: http://www.ratemyprofessors.com/About.jsp.

Rempel, J. K., Holmes, J. G., & Zanna, M. P. (1985). Trust in close relationships. *Journal of Personality and Social Psychology*, *49*, 95–112.

Resnick, P., & Zeckhauser, R. (2001). Trust among strangers in Internet transactions: Empirical analysis of eBay's reputation system. Retrieved March 29, 2006 from: http://www.si.umich.edu/Bpresnick.

Resnick, P., Zeckhauser, R., Friedman, E., & Kuwabara, K. (2000). Reputation systems. *Communications of the ACM*, *43* (12), 45–48.

Rice, R. E., & Love, G. (1987). Electronic emotion: Socioemotional content in a computer mediated communication network. *Communication Research*, *14*, 85–108.

Riegelsberger, J., & Sasse, M. A. (2001). Trust builders and trustbusters: The role of trust cues in interfaces to e-commerce applications. In *Towards the E-Society: Proceedings of the First IFIP Conference on E-Commerce, E-Society, and E-Government* (pp. 17–30). London: Kluwer.

Riegelsberger, J., Sasse, M. A., & McCarthy, J. (2003). The researcher's dilemma: Evaluating trust in computer-mediated communication. *International Journal of Human Computer Studies*, *58* (6), 759–781.

Robinson, R., & West, R. (1992). A comparison of computer and questionnaire methods of history-taking in a genito-urinary clinic. *Psychology and Health*, *6*, 77–84.

Rochlen, A. B., Beretvas, S. N., & Zack, J. S. (2004). The online and face-to-face counseling attitudes scales: A validation study. *Measurement and Evaluation in Counseling and Development*, *3*, 95–111.

Rogers, C. (1951). *Client-centered therapy*. Boston: Houghton-Mifflin.

Roscoe, B., Cavanaugh, L., & Kennedy, D. (1988). Dating infidelity: Behaviors reasons, and consequences. *Adolescence*, *23*, 35–43.

Rotter, J. B. (1967). A new scale for the measurement of interpersonal trust. *Journal of Personality*, *35*, 651–665.

Rubin, Z. (1975). Disclosing oneself to a stranger: Reciprocity and its limits. *Journal of Experimental Social Psychology*, *11*, 233–260.

SA Crimes Act, Office of the South Australian Attorney-General. s562A. 31 August 2001.

Sander, F. (1996). Couples group therapy conducted via computer-mediated communication: A preliminary case study. *Computers in Human Behavior*, *12* (2), 301–312.

Sanders, C. E., Field, T. M. Diego, M., & Kaplan, M. (2000). The relationship of Internet use to depression and social isolation among adolescents. *Adolescence*, *35* (138), 237–242.

Sassenberg, K., Boos, M., & Rabung, S. (2005). Attitude change in face to face and computer-mediated communication: Private self-awareness as mediator and moderator. *European Journal of Social Psychology, 35,* 361–374.

Savicki, V., Lingenfelter, D., & Kelley, M. (1996). Gender language style and group composition in Internet discussion lists. *Journal of Computer Mediated Communication, 2* (3).

Scharlott, B. W., & Christ, W. G. (1995). Overcoming relationship-initiation barriers: The impact of a computer-dating system on sex role, shyness, and appearance inhibitions. *Computers in Human Behavior, 11,* 191–204.

Schatz Byford, K. (1996). Privacy in cyberspace: Constructing a model of privacy for the electronic communications environment. *Rutgers Computer and Technology Law Journal, 24,* 1–74.

Schelling, T. C. (1968). Game theory and the study of ethical systems. *The Journal of Conflict Resolution, 12* (1), 34–44.

Schoeman, F. (1984). Privacy and intimate information. In F. Schoeman (Ed.), *Philosophical dimensions of privacy* (pp. 403–417). Cambridge: Cambridge University Press.

Shackelford, T., & Buss D. (1996). Betrayal in mateships, friendships, and coalitions. *Journal of Personality and Social Psychology, 22,* 1151–1164.

Shackelford, T. K., Voracek, M., Schmitt, D. P., Buss, D. M., Weekes-Shackelford, V. A., & Michalski, R. L. (2004). Romantic jealousy in early adulthood in later life. *Human Nature, 15* (3), 59–76.

Sharf, B. (1997). Communication breast cancer online: Support and empowerment on the Internet. *Women and Health, 26,* 65–84.

Sharp, H. (2005). Phone technology aids UAE dating. *BBC News,* 29 July. Retrieved August 16, 2006 from: http://news.bbc.co.uk/1/hi/world/middle_east/4718697.stm.

Shaw, J. (1997). Treatment rationale for internet infidelity. *Journal of Sex Education and Therapy, 22* (1), 29–34.

Sheppard, V., Nelson, E., & Andreoli-Mathie, V. (1995). Dating relationships and infidelity: Attitudes and behaviors. *Journal of Sex and Marital Therapy, 21* (3), 202–212.

Sheridan, L., Davies, G., & Boon, J. (2002). The course and nature of stalking: A victim perspective, *Howard Journal, 40* (3), 215–234.

Short, J., Williams, E., & Christie, B. (1976). *The social psychology of telecommunications.* Chichester: Wiley.

Sillence, E., Briggs, P., Fishwick, L., & Harris, P. (2004). Trust and mistrust of online health sites. In *Proceedings of the Conference on Human Factors in Computing Systems* (pp. 663–670), 24–29 April. Vienna, Austria. New York: ACM Press.

Sillence, E., Briggs, P., Harris, P., & Fishwick, L. (2006). Changes in online health usage over the last five years. In *Proceedings of the Conference on Human Factors in Computing Systems.* Montréal, Canada, 22–27 April.

Sillence, E., Briggs, P., Harris, P. R., & Fishwick, L. (2007). How do patients evaluate and make use of online health information? *Social Science and Medicine, 64,* 1853–1862.

Sillence, E., Briggs, P. Harris, P. R., & Fishwick, L. (2006). A framework for understanding trust factors in web based health advice. *International Journal of Human Computer Studies, 64* (8), 697–713.

Smh.com.au (2006). Online bidders cautious. August. Retrieved September 15, 2006 from: cautious/2006/08/16/1155407816374.html.

Smith, J. H., Milberg, S. J., & Burke, S. J. (1996). Information privacy: Measuring individuals concerns about organizational practices. *MIS Quarterly, June,* 167–196.

Smyth, J. M. (1998). Written emotional expression: effect sizes, outcome, types, and moderating variables. *Journal of Consulting and Clinical Psychology, 66,* 174–184.

Sobel, D. L. (2000). The process that 'John Doe' is due: Addressing the legal challenge to Internet anonymity. *Virginia Journal of Law and Technology, 5,* 1522–1687.

Sparck-Jones, K. (2003). Privacy: What's different now? *Interdisciplinary Science Reviews, 28,* 287–292.

Spiekermann, S., Grossklags, J., & Berendt, B. (2001). E-privacy in 2nd generation e-commerce: Privacy preferences versus actual behavior. In *Proceedings of the Third ACM Conference on Electronic Commerce, Association for Computing Machinery* (pp. 38–47). Tampa, FL.

Spitzberg, B. H. (2002). The tactical topography of stalking victimization and management. *Trauma, Violence, and Abuse, 3* (4), 261–288.

Spitzberg, B. H., & Cupach, W. R. (2002). The inappropriateness of relational intrusion. In R. Goodwin & D. Cramer (Eds), *Inappropriate relationships: The unconventional, the disapproved, and the forbidden* (pp. 191–219). Mahwah, NJ: Lawrence Erlbaum Associates, Inc.

Spitzberg, B. H., & Cupach, W. R. (2003). What mad pursuit? Conceptualization and assessment of obsessive relational intrusion and stalking-related phenomena. *Aggression and Violent Behavior: A Review Journal, 8,* 345–375.

Spitzberg, B. H., & Hoobler, G. (2002). Cyberstalking and the technologies of interpersonal terrorism. *New Media and Society, 14,* 67–88.

Sproull, L., & Kiesler, S. (1986). Reducing social context cues: Electronic mail in organizational communication. *Management Science, 32,* 1492–1512.

Sproull, L., Subramani, M., Kiesler, S., Walker, J. H., & Waters, K. (1996). When the interface is a face. *Human–Computer Interaction, 11,* 97–124.

Spytech online. (n.d.). Retrieved March 29, 2006 from: http://www.spytech-web.com/spouse-monitoring.shtml.

Stanford, J., Tauber, E. R., Fogg, B. J., & Marable, L. (2002). Experts vs. online consumers: A comparative credibility study of health and finance web sites. Retrieved March 29, 2006 from: http://www.consumerwebwatch.org/news/report3 credibilityresearch/slicedbreadabstract.htm.

Stofle, G. S. (2002). Chat room therapy. In R. C. Hsiung (Ed.), *e-Therapy: Case studies, guiding principles, and the clinical potential of the internet* (pp. 92–135). New York: Norton.

Stofle, G. S., & Chchele, P. J. (2004). Online counseling skills, Part II: In-session skills. In R. Kraus, J. S. Zack, & G. Stricker (Eds), *Online counselling: A handbook for mental health professionals* (pp. 182–196). San Diego, CA: Elsevier Academic Press.

Stuttaford, T. (2006). Romance with a keyboard. *The Times,* 10 June. Retrieved June 25, 2006 from: http://www.timesonline.co.uk/article/0,,8123-2217209,00.html.

Suler, J. R. (2000). Psychotherapy in cyberspace: A 5-dimension model of online and computer-mediated psychotherapy. *CyberPsychology and Behavior*, *3*, 151–160.

Suler, J. (2001). Assessing a person's suitability for online therapy. *CyberPsychology and Behavior*, *4* (6), 675–679.

Suler, J. (2004a). The online disinhibition effect. *CyberPsychology and Behavior*, *7*, 321–326.

Suler, J. (2004b). The psychology of text relationships. In R. Kraus, J. S. Zack, & G. Stricker (Eds), *Online counselling: A handbook for mental health professionals* (pp. 51–68). San Diego, CA: Elsevier Academic Press.

Suler, J. R. (2004c). Psychotherapy in cyberspace: A 5-dimension model of online and computer-mediated psychotherapy. *Psychology of cyberspace* (internet book). Retrieved March 7, 2005 from: http://www.rider.edu/~suler/psycyber/therapy. html.

Tanis, M., & Postmes, T. (2007). Two faces of anonymity: Paradoxical effects of cues to identity in CMC. *Computers in Human Behavior*, *23*, 955–970.

The Register (2006). The hive mind has spoken: 'I need help!' Retrieved October 31, 2006 from: http://www.theregister.co.uk/2005/09/22/blogging_is_therapy.

Thibaut, J., & Kelley, H. (1959). *The social psychology of groups.* New York: Wiley.

Thompsen, P. A. (1994). An episode of flaming: A creative narrative. *ETC: A Review of General Semantics*, *51*, 51–72.

Thompsen, P. A., & Foulger, D. A. (1996). Effects of pictographs and quoting on flaming in electronic mail. *Computers in Human Behavior*, *12*, 225–243.

Thomson, R., & Murachver, T. (2001). Predicting gender from electronic discourse. *British Journal of Social Psychology*, *40*, 193–208.

Tidwell, L. C., & Walther, J. B. (2002). Computer-mediated communication effects on disclosure, impressions, and interpersonal evaluations: Getting to know one another a bit at a time. *Human Communication Research*, *28*, 317–348.

Tourangeau, R. (2004). Survey research and societal change. *Annual Review of Psychology*, *55*, 775–801.

Tourangeau, R., Couper, M. P., & Steiger, D. M. (2003). Humanizing self-administered surveys: Experiments on social presence in web and IVR surveys. *Computers in Human Behaviour*, *19*, 1–24.

Tourangeau, R., & Smith, T. W. (1996). Asking sensitive questions: The impact of data collection mode, question format, and question context. *Public Opinion Quarterly*, *60*, 275–304.

Townsend, J., & Levy, G. (1990). Effects of potential partners' costume and physical attractiveness on sexuality and partner selection. *Journal of Psychology*, *124*, 371–389.

Trevino, L., Lengel, R., & Daft, R. (1987). Media symbolism, media richness, and media choice in organizations: A symbolic interactionist perspective. *Communication Research*, *14*, 553–574.

Turkle, S. (1995). *Life on the screen: Identity in the age of the internet.* London: Weidenfeld & Nicolson.

US Attorney General (1999). *Cyberstalking: A new challenge for law enforcement and industry*. Report from the Attorney General to the Vice President, August. Retrieved July 18, 2004 from: http://www.usdoj.gov/criminal/cybercrime/cyber stalking.htm.

Utz, S. (2000). Social information processing in MUDs: The development of friendships in virtual worlds. *Journal of Online Behavior, 1* (1). Retrieved February 7, 2005 from: http://www.behavior.net/JOB/v1n1/utz.html.

Utz, S. (2005). Types of deception and underlying. motivation: What people think. *Social Science Computer Review, 23,* 49–56.

Valkenburg, P. M., Schouten, A. P., & Peter, J. (2005). Adolescents' identity experiments on the Internet. *New Media and Society, 7,* 383–402.

VandenBos, G. R., & Williams, S. (2000). The Internet versus the telephone: What is telehealth, anyway? *Professional Psychology: Research and Practice, 31* (5), 490–492.

Van Gelder, L. (1991). The strange case of the electronic lover. In C. Dunlop & R. Kling (Eds), *Computerization and controversy: Value conflicts and social choice.* Boston, MA: Academic Press.

Vasalou, A., Pitt, J., & Joinson, A. (2006). The role of shame, guilt and embarrassment in online social dilemmas. *Proceedings of BHCI.* London, Queen Mary's College, September.

Walther, J. B. (1992). Interpersonal effects in computer-mediated interaction: A relational perspective. *Communication Research, 19* (1), 52–90.

Walther, J. B. (1995). Relational aspects of computer-mediated communication: Experimental observations over time. *Organizational Science, 6,* 186–203.

Walther, J. B. (1996). Computer-mediated communication: Impersonal, interpersonal and hyperpersonal interaction. *Communication Research, 23,* 3–43.

Walther, J. B. (1999). Visual cues and computer-mediated communication: Don't look before you leap. Paper presented at the Annual Meeting of the International Communication Association, May, San Francisco.

Walther, J. B. (2002). Research ethics in Internet-enabled research: Human subjects issues and methodological myopia. *Ethics and Information Technology, 4* (3), 205–216.

Walther, J. B., Slovacek, C., & Tidwell, L. (1999). Is a picture worth a thousand words? Photographic image in long-term and short-term virtual teams. Paper presented at the Annual Meeting of the International Communication Association, May, San Francisco.

Walther, J. B., Slovacek, C., & Tidwell, L. (2001). Is a picture worth a thousand words? Photographic images in long-term and short-term computer-mediated communication. *Communication Research, 28,* 105–134.

Walther, J. B., Van Der Heide, B., Kim, S., Westerman, D., & Tong, S. T. (2008). The role of friends' appearance and behavior on evaluations of individuals on facebook: Are we known by the company we keep? *Human Communication Research, 34* (1), 28–49.

Wang, Y. D., & Emurian, H. H. (2005). An overview of online trust: Concepts, elements, and implications. *Computers in Human Behavior, 21,* 105–125.

Warren, S., & Brandeis, L. (1890). The right to privacy. *Harvard Law Review, 4* (5), 193–200.

Watson, R. T., Akselsen, S., & Pitt, L. F. (1998). Attractors: Building mountains in the flat landscape of the World Wide Web. *California Management Review, 40* (2), 36–56.

Weisband, S., & Kiesler, S. (1996). Self-disclosure on computer forms: Meta-analysis and implications. *Proceedings of CHI96.* Retrieved June 20, 2005 from: http://www.acm.org/sigchi/chi96/proceedings/papers/Weisband/sw_txt.htm.

Weiser, M. (1988). Ubiquitous computing. Retrieved March 19, 2006 from: http://

www.ubiq.com/hypertext/weiser/UbiHome.html. Originally published at Xerox PARC, 1988.

Weiss, P. (2006). What a tangled web we weave: Being googled can jeopardize your job search. *Daily News: The Front Page*, 19 March. Retrieved March 19, 2006 from: http://www.nydailynews.com/front/story/401069p-339405c.html.

Wellman, B. (1997). An electronic group is virtually a social network. In S. Kielser (Ed.), *Culture of the internet* (pp. 179–205). Mahwah, NJ: Lawrence Erlbaum Associates, Inc.

Westin, A. (1967). *Privacy and freedom*. New York: Atheneum.

Whitty, M. T. (2002a). Liar, liar! An examination of how open, supportive and honest people are in chat rooms. *Computers in Human Behavior*, *18*, 343–352.

Whitty, M. T. (2002b). *Big brother in Australia: Privacy and surveillance of the internet in the Australian workplace*. Paper presented at the Internet Research 3.0: Net/Work/Theory, Maastricht, the Netherlands, 13–16 October.

Whitty, M. T. (2003a). Cyber-flirting: Playing at love on the internet. *Theory and Psychology*, *13*, 339–357.

Whitty, M. T. (2003b). Pushing the wrong buttons: Men's and women's attitudes towards online and offline infidelity. *CyberPsychology and Behavior*, *6*, 569–579.

Whitty, M. T. (2004a). Peering into online bedroom windows: Considering the ethical implications of investigating Internet relationships and sexuality. In E. Buchanan (Ed.), *Readings in virtual research ethics: Issues and controversies* (pp. 203–218). Hershey: Idea Group Inc.

Whitty, M. T. (2004b). Should filtering software be utilised in the workplace? Australian employee's attitudes towards internet usage and surveillance of the internet in the workplace. *Surveillance and Society*, *2* (1), 39–54.

Whitty, M. T. (2004c). Cyber-flirting: An examination of men's and women's flirting behaviour both offline and on the Internet. *Behaviour Change*, *21* (2), 115–126.

Whitty, M. T. (2005). The 'realness' of cyber-cheating: Men and women's representations of unfaithful Internet relationships. *Social Science Computer Review*, *23* (1), 57–67.

Whitty, M. T. (2007a). The art of selling one's self on an online dating site: The BAR approach. In M. T. Whitty, A. J. Baker, & J. A. Inman (Eds), *Online matchmaking* (pp. 57–69). Basingstoke: Palgrave Macmillan.

Whitty, M. T. (2007b). Conclusion. In M. T. Whitty, A. J. Baker, & J. A. Inman (Eds), *Online matchmaking* (pp. 197–201). Basingstoke: Palgrave Macmillan.

Whitty, M. T. (2007c). Manipulation of self in cyberspace. In B. H. Spitzberg & W. R. Cupach, *The dark side of interpersonal communication* (2nd ed.) (pp. 93–118). Mahwah, NJ: Lawrence Erlbaum Associates, Inc.

Whitty, M. T. (2008). Revealing the 'real' me, searching for the 'actual' you: Presentations of self on an internet dating site. *Computers in Human Behavior*, *24*, 1707–1723.

Whitty, M. T., & Buchanan, T. (in press). Looking for love in so many places: Characteristics of online daters and speed daters. *Interpersona: An International Journal on Personal Relationships*.

Whitty, M. T., & Carr, A. N. (2005a). Taking the good with the bad: Applying Klein's work to further our understanding of cyber-cheating. *Journal of Couple and Relationship Therapy: Special issue on Treating Infidelity*, *4* (2/3), 103–115.

Whitty, M. T., & Carr, A. N. (2005b). Electronic bullying in the workplace. In B.

Fisher, V. Bowie, & C. Cooper (Eds), *Workplace violence* (pp. 103–115). Uffculme: Willan.

Whitty, M. T., & Carr, A. N. (2006a). *Cyberspace romance: The psychology of online relationships*. Basingstoke: Palgrave Macmillan.

Whitty, M. T., & Carr, A. N. (2006b). New rules in the workplace: Applying object-relations theory to explain problem Internet and email behavior in the workplace. *Computers in Human Behavior, 22* (2), 235–250.

Whitty, M. T., & Carville, S. E. (2008). Would I lie to you? Self-serving lies and other-oriented lies told across different media. *Computers in Human Behavior, 24* (4), 1707–1723.

Whitty, M., & Gavin, J. (2001). Age/sex/location: Uncovering the social cues in the development of online relationships. *CyberPsychology and Behaviour, 4*, 623–630.

Whitty, M. T., & McLaughlin, D. (2007). Online recreation: The relationship between loneliness, internet self-efficacy and the use of the internet for entertainment purposes. *Computers in Human Behavior, 23* (3), 1435–1446.

Whitty, M. T., & Quigley, L. (in press). Emotional and sexual infidelity offline and in cyberspace. *Journal of Marital and Family Therapy*.

Williams, P., Huntington, P., & Nicholas, D. (2003). Health information on the Internet: A qualitative study of NHS direct online users. *Aslib Proceedings, 55* (5/6), 304–312.

Winzelberg, A. (1997). The analysis of an electronic support group for individuals with eating disorders. *Computers in Human Behavior, 13* (3), 393–407.

Wiretap Professional 6.0. (n.d.). Retrieved March 29, 2006 from: http://www.wiretappro.com/.

Wolak, J., Mitchell, K. J., & Finkelhor, D. (2003). Escaping or connecting? Characteristics of youth who form close online relationships. *Journal of Adolescence, 26*, 105–119.

Wright, J., & Chung, M. C. (2001). Mastery or mystery? Therapeutic writing: A review of the literature. *British Journal of Guidance and Counselling, 29*, 277–291.

Wu, M., Miller, R. C., & Garfinkel, S. L. (2006). Do security toolbars actually prevent phishing attacks? In *Proceedings of the SIGCHI Conference on Human Factors in Computing Systems*. New York: ACM Press.

Wysocki, D. K. (1998). Let your fingers to do the talking: Sex on an adult chat-line. *Sexualities, 1*, 425–452.

Yager, J. (2001). E-mail as a therapeutic adjunct in the outpatient treatment of anorexia nervosa: Illustrative case material and discussion of the issues. *International Journal of Eating Disorders, 29* (2), 125–138.

Yarab, P. E., & Allgeier, E. (1998). Don't even think about it: The role of sexual fantasies as perceived unfaithfulness in heterosexual dating relationships. *Journal of Sex Education and Therapy, 23* (3), 246–254.

Yarab, P. E., Sensibaugh, C. C., & Allgeier, E. (1998). More than just sex: Gender differences in the incidence of self-defined unfaithful behavior in heterosexual dating relationships. *Journal of Psychology and Human Sexuality, 10* (2), 45–57.

Young, K. S. (1998). Internet addiction: The emergence of a new clinical disorder. *CyberPsychology and Behavior, 1*, 237–244.

Young, K. S., Griffin-Shelley, E., Cooper, A., O'Mara, J., & Buchanan, J. (2000). Online infidelity: A new dimension in couple relationships with implications for evaluation and treatment. *Sexual Addiction and Compulsivity, 7*, 59–74.

Yurchisin, J., Watchravesringkan, K., & Mccabe, D. B. (2005). An exploration of identity re-creation in the context of internet dating. *Social Behavior and Personality: An International Journal, 33* (8), 735–750.

Zelvin, E., & Speyer, C. M. (2004). Online counselling skills, part 1: Treatment strategies and skills for conducting counselling online. In R. Kraus, J. S. Zack, & G. Stricker (Eds), *Online counselling: A handbook for mental health professionals* (pp. 163–180). San Diego, CA: Elsevier Academic Press.

Zheng, J., Bos, N. D., Olson, J. S., & Olson, G. M. (2001). Trust without touch: Jump-start trust with social chat. In *Proceedings of the Conference on Human Factors in Computing Systems* (pp. 291–292). New York: ACM Press.

Zhou, L., Burgoon, J. K., Nunamaker, J. F., & Twitchell, D. (2004). Automating linguistics-based cues for detecting deception in text-based asynchronous computer-mediated communication. *Group Decision and Negotiation, 13*, 81–106.

Zuckoff, M. (2006). The perfect Mark: How a Massachusetts psychotherapist fell for a Nigerian e-mail scam. *The New Yorker*, 8 May. Retrieved October 3, 2006 from: http://www.newyorker.com/archive/2006/05/15/060515fa_fact.

Author index

Subject index